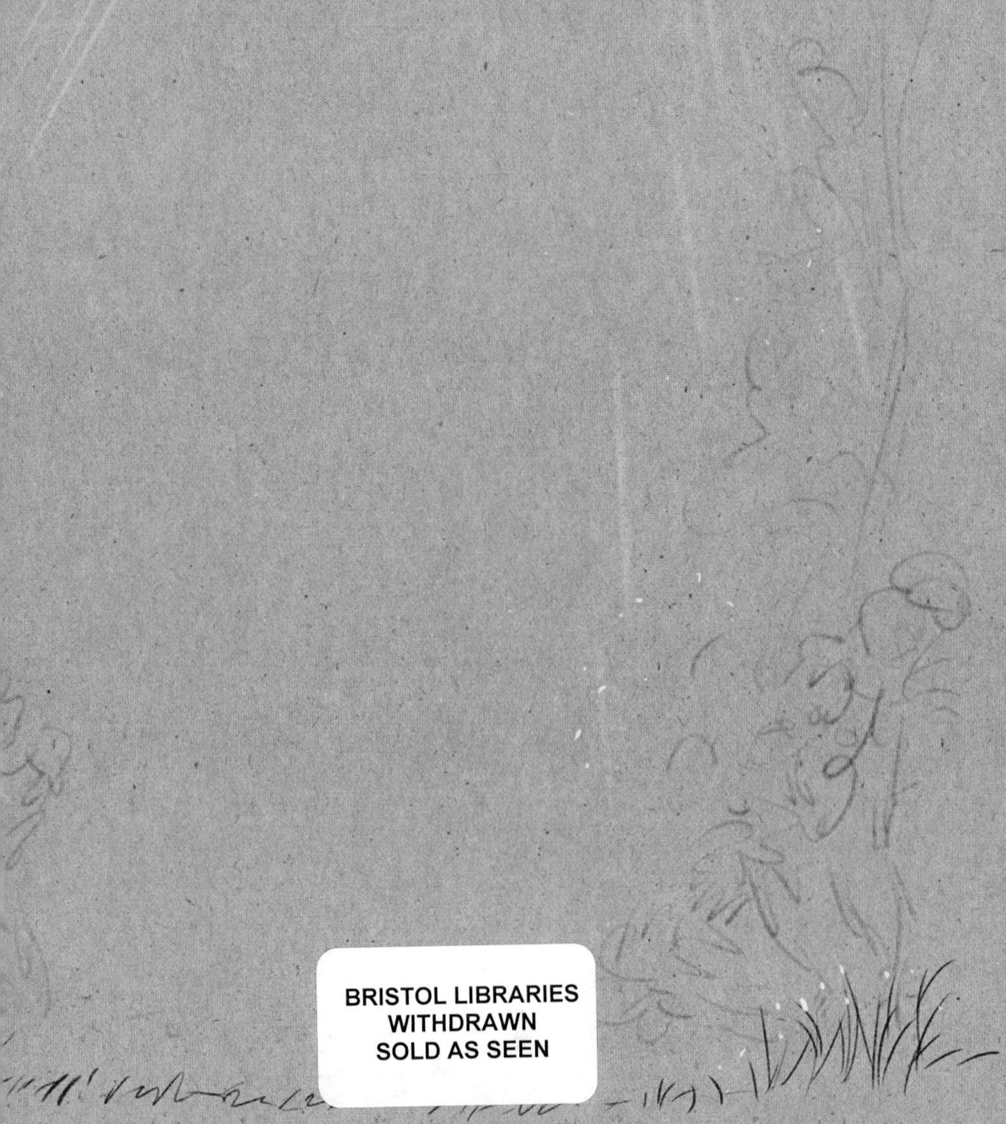

Born in 1961, Gary Andrews graduated from Exeter College of Art & Design in 1983, at which point he landed a career in animation. Over the years he has worked on many commercials and pop promos, had a spell at Disney, animated several Beatrix Potter characters as well as Toad from *The Wind in the Willows*. He has directed *Fireman Sam* and *Horrid Henry* and is also a prolific illustrator, often to be seen in the pages of *Private Eye*, where he has been illustrating the 'Sylvie Krin' stories for over thirty years.

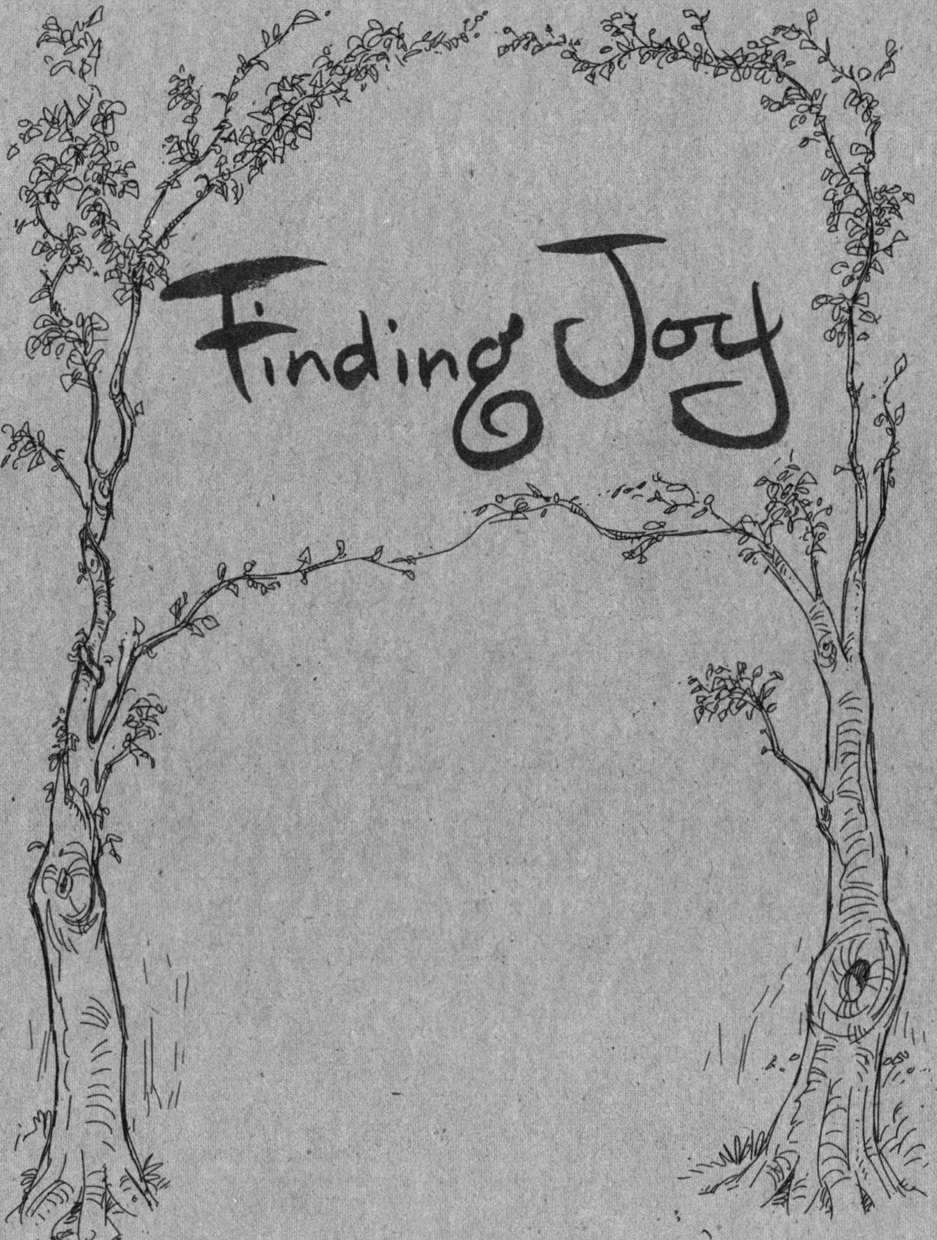
Finding Joy

Finding Joy

Gary Andrews

JOHN MURRAY

First published in Great Britain in 2020 by John Murray (Publishers)
An Hachette UK company

1

Text and illustrations copyright © Gary Andrews 2020

A CIP catalogue record for this title is available from the British Library

Hardback ISBN 978-1-529-33813-3
eBook ISBN 978-1-529-33814-0

Typeset in LaskiSlab by Chris Callard at beachstone.co.uk

Printed and Bound in Italy by L.E.G.O. SpA

John Murray policy is to use papers that are natural, renewable and recyclable
products and made from wood grown in sustainable forests. The logging and
manufacturing processes are expected to conform to the environmental regulations
of the country of origin.

John Murray (Publishers)
Carmelite House
50 Victoria Embankment
London EC4Y oDZ

www.johnmurraypress.co.uk

About this book

I would be very happy if this book had never been. I was quite content drawing a daily doodle diary as a record of our life that was seen by my wife Joy and our kids and the few friends who followed me on social media.

All that changed when Joy died unexpectedly in 2017. Then the drawings took on another purpose. They became a form of self-counselling – a moment of meditation at the end of each day as I tried to make sense of my grief and the changes to my life. I kept posting them, mainly for my friends to know how I was doing. What I never expected was how they would resonate with a wider audience – that they would come to mean so much to so many people.

From very early on I was often asked, 'Are you going to make a book out of them?' Well, it would appear that the answer is yes. This is not a 'how to grieve' manual; I don't claim to be an expert or have any magic solutions. It is simply one man's experience in coming to terms with widowerhood and navigating life's twists and turns as a solo parent. I hope it will help others in a similar position and, in the process, raise the odd smile too.

I am writing this note in a world in lockdown, where many millions of people have had their old lives whisked away and are trying to find a new way forward. To steer a course through grief and isolation, what we all need – and what keeps us human – is love.

Finding Joy is the legacy of a love I was privileged to know, and I am honoured to share a bit of that love in these pages.

Gary Andrews
April 2020

Introduction

I first noticed Joy in February 1992.

I was sitting in the back row of a performance by the Archway Theatre – a small, local amateur company I had recently joined. A tall, striking, dark-haired young woman was on the stage performing a comedy sketch about someone waking up and trying to get ready to go to work. She was brilliant.

Fast-forward six years. I was directing a production of *A Midsummer Night's Dream* at the same theatre and had cast Joy as Helena. She was an obvious choice: apart from her comic timing and excellent acting skills, at a whisker under six feet tall she was perfect for Shakespeare's 'painted maypole'! During the course of this show we very quickly became close friends, with a shared sense of humour and a love of Shakespeare at the core of that friendship. I didn't kid myself that it could ever be anything more than just a friendship – after all, she was gorgeous, and I was fifteen years older as well as several inches shorter. I was just happy to hang out with her.

Over the next few months Joy and I saw more and more of each other and then, one wonderful day, we were sitting in her flat watching a film. We turned to each other to say something and our eyes met.

Suddenly we both experienced the same feeling: a tumbling, falling sensation that we later called our 'Stargate moment'. We kissed and that was it ... it soon became very clear that we wanted to spend the rest of our lives together.

On New Year's Eve 2002 I asked her if she would become my wife. She said yes and in September 2004 we were married. I was the happiest man in the world.

In 2007 our daughter Lily was born. I was by now a director, working in children's animated TV, and Joy decided to put her acting career on hold and concentrate on being a mum. Life was pretty idyllic. In 2010 Joy gave birth to our son Ben, and our little family was complete.

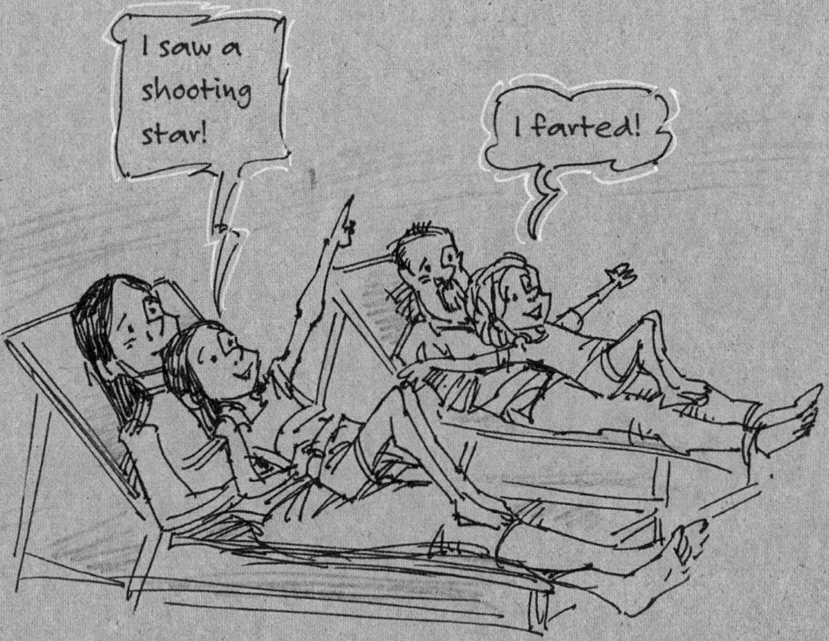
I saw a shooting star!
I farted!

Can we swap?

In October 2017 I was due to fly to Vancouver on business for a week, so we spent the weekend together as a family in Glastonbury at a faery festival. We enjoyed two days catching up with lovely friends, going to the pub and listening to folk music – it could not have been more perfect. It would be the last weekend we would spend together.

On Monday, 23 October, we took the long drive to Heathrow, stopping off in Cheddar Gorge to stretch our legs and have a last look at the beautiful countryside. We made good time and Joy and the kids came to the airport to see me off. We shared a sandwich and kissed goodbye. By the time I checked in at my hotel in Vancouver, they were asleep in bed and so I turned in myself, looking forward to seeing them again the following week.

Early the next morning I FaceTimed Joy. She answered, looking pale and tired.

'You OK?' I asked.

'No,' she replied, 'I think I've got the flu.'

'Oh no – you always get poorly when I go away! Make sure you get lots of rest.'

We said goodbye and I got on with my work.

The next day I called again. She was on the sofa in our living room, still smiling but no better. As it was half-term the kids had gone to Gran'ma for the day to give her a break, and she was sitting with the dog on her lap watching TV. She was sure that all she needed was some rest. I told her I loved her and would call again the next day, when her sister was due to arrive from France to stay for a few days.

Thursday came and I texted, as always, to see if it was a good time to talk. The reply came: 'NOT REALLY. CALL LILY.' Puzzled, I FaceTimed Lily.

'Is everything all right?'

'Mummy still feels poorly. Aunty Marie has called the doctor.'

I told her to give Joy and Marie my love, that everything would be OK and to keep me posted. Later that day I was at lunch when my phone rang. It was Marie.

'Joy has been taken to hospital. The doctor thinks she may have a kidney infection. She'll probably have to stay overnight.'

About an hour later the phone rang again.

'They think it's quite serious. Can you get an early flight home?'

I set about changing my flight immediately, imagining I would need to look after the kids while Joy stayed in hospital for a few days. I had just finished sorting it out when another call came. It was Marie again, asking if I had managed to get the flight – Joy was not at all well. There was a catch in her voice that set alarm bells ringing. I assured her I was due on a plane that night and would be home by lunchtime on Friday.

That flight was the longest of my life. I couldn't concentrate on anything and had no appetite so simply closed my eyes and dozed fitfully. When I landed, I was surprised to see Joy's mother and her eldest brother waiting for me at the gate; I assumed they had come to take me directly to the hospital to see Joy.

When we got to the car Joy's mum told me the news: despite all the best efforts of the hospital team, Joy had died at 3.15 that morning. I was numb. This wasn't right. I was the older one – it was me who was supposed to die first. She was young, fit, full of life… it made no sense. At that moment it was still unclear why she had died – it would take a post-mortem to establish the cause was multiple organ failure as a result of sepsis.

They told me that they had managed to keep the news from the kids as they thought I would want to be the one to tell them. When we arrived home we found Lily and Ben playing in the small park opposite our house. They were very pleased to see me and I hugged them and took them into the garden.

What followed was the hardest thing I have ever had to do, as I held them close and told them that Mummy had died. As long as I live, I will never forget their animal howls of pain as the news sank in. We held each other and cried. After a while we went inside and I began the task of letting everyone else know.

Later that night, as I eventually contemplated getting into bed (where my two children were asleep, unable to settle in their own beds), I knew I had to post my doodle. Since my fifty-fifth birthday I had kept a doodle diary and I drew every day. I had always shown each finished drawing to Joy and we had laughed together or chatted about it. I knew she would be disappointed if I stopped. But that night all I could draw was a broken heart.

The first weekend was all about just getting through.
There was a strange calm – it all seemed so unreal…

… but on the Sunday night, watching *Strictly Come Dancing* (usually a 'Mummy and the kids' experience), the dam broke.

A visit from two close friends the next evening, and finally it was my turn for the floodgates to open.

Joy's cremation signified the end of her physical presence and allowed me to move forward on my journey to healing. I began to come to terms with the fact that she was truly gone.

We held a Passing Ceremony for her in the woods, and as we said goodbye a shaft of sunlight broke through the trees. It was beautiful.

From that day on, I felt I could talk to Joy again – that she was all around me.

Life carried on in its own strange, new way.

'Breakfast.

Strip beds.

Take Ben to tennis.

Get props from the loft for play.

Vacuum house.

Pick up online orders.

Lunch at Gran'ma's.

Big shop!

Make beds.

Whisky and TV.

Watch play.

Cook dinner.

I have been getting used to my new life as a widower for around a week now, and if ever anyone says to me that 'stay-at-home' mums have it easy... I will punch them in the face.

Explaining the new system by which we now need to
live our lives.

Had my first double play date today… and survived it!

Every day we learned a little more how to process this new life...

... each in our own, sometimes surprising, ways.

And things slowly went back to a semblance of normal . . .

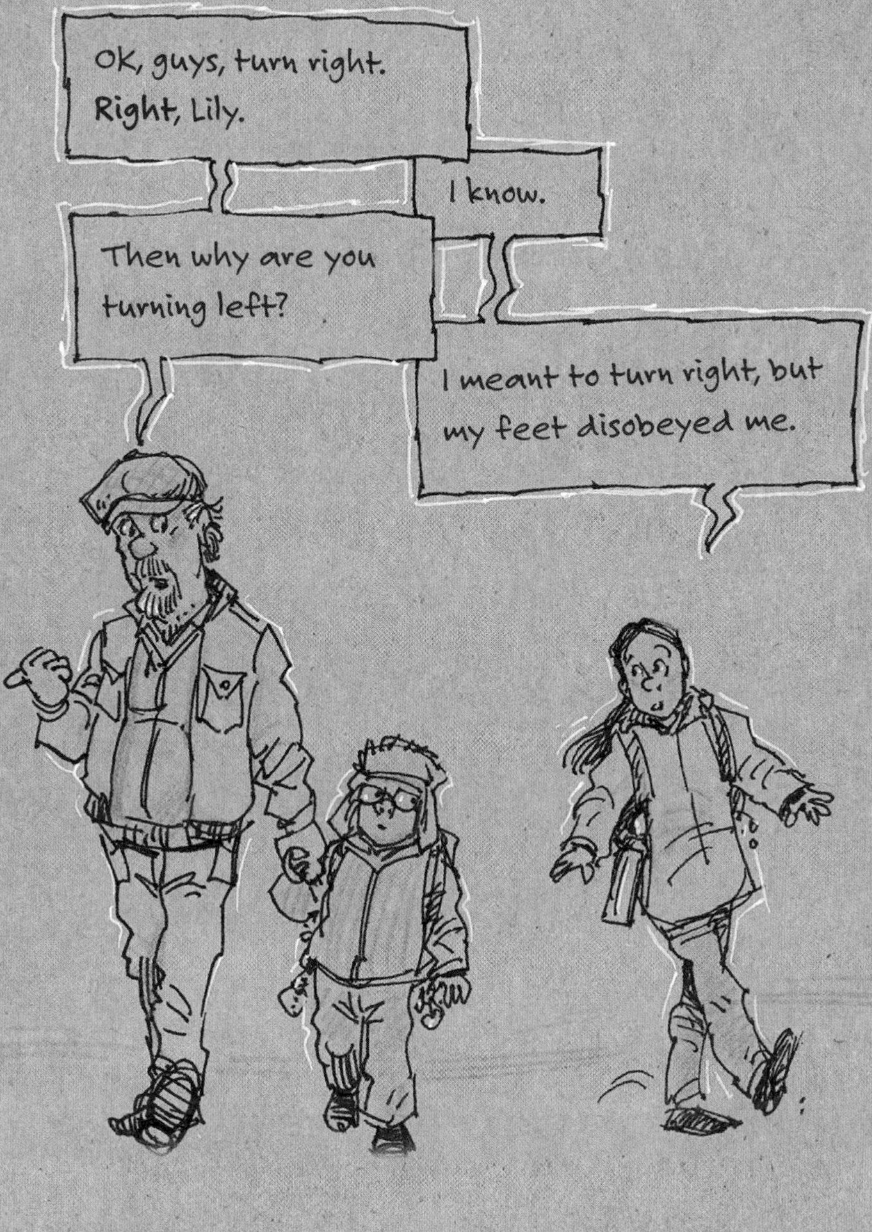
Ok, guys, turn right. Right, Lily.
I know.
Then why are you turning left?
I meant to turn right, but my feet disobeyed me.

... even though 'normal' had been irrevocably changed.

It was clear that Lily and Ben both craved closeness and reassurance.

I love the fact we have an enormous sofa and yet you choose to sit there.

But once they were both asleep, the loneliness would hit me – hard.

The sofa feels very big and very empty.

The first Christmas was a challenge. In some ways it was the same as always.

We carried on old traditions, like carol singing at our local theatre.

With family staying, and visitors dropping by, everyone was trying to keep up a sense of wonder and magic.

It was only when Christmas Day itself had passed that I felt the emptiness at the heart of our celebrations.

But we got there.

Great work, team!

And I saw in the New Year with a new confidence,
grateful for the friends and family around me.

Up until Christmas, the kids hadn't really cried very much since I first told them the news. Lily, in particular, found it hard to cry…

...but with the New Year came the realisation that this new life was for keeps.

We planted a tree for Joy and buried some of her ashes.

It marked a turning point for us, as we began to look to the future. Contemplating life without my best friend, with whom it had all made sense, was overwhelming at times.

Yet life kept moving forward, and I started to find joy in small, everyday moments.

Impromptu snowball fight.

All three of us were learning to be happy again . . .

Bedtime or, as we called it tonight, climbing the north face of the Eiger.

*Our new Friday ritual. Ben loves it
(and I get to read for ninety minutes!).*

... although some things would never change.

The days would often fall into a rhythm...

Another week over. All clean. All fed. Jobs done.
Tick-tock, tick-tock.

. . . until the grief was brought back by a question,

or a place,

I know I need to go to bed…
but it's the emptiest place in
the world.

or finding something that Joy would have loved . . .

or, sometimes, by nothing at all.

The next few months had their ups and downs…

...but it never failed to amaze me how the kids handled life's new challenges.

Lily's strength was extraordinary, especially for one so young.

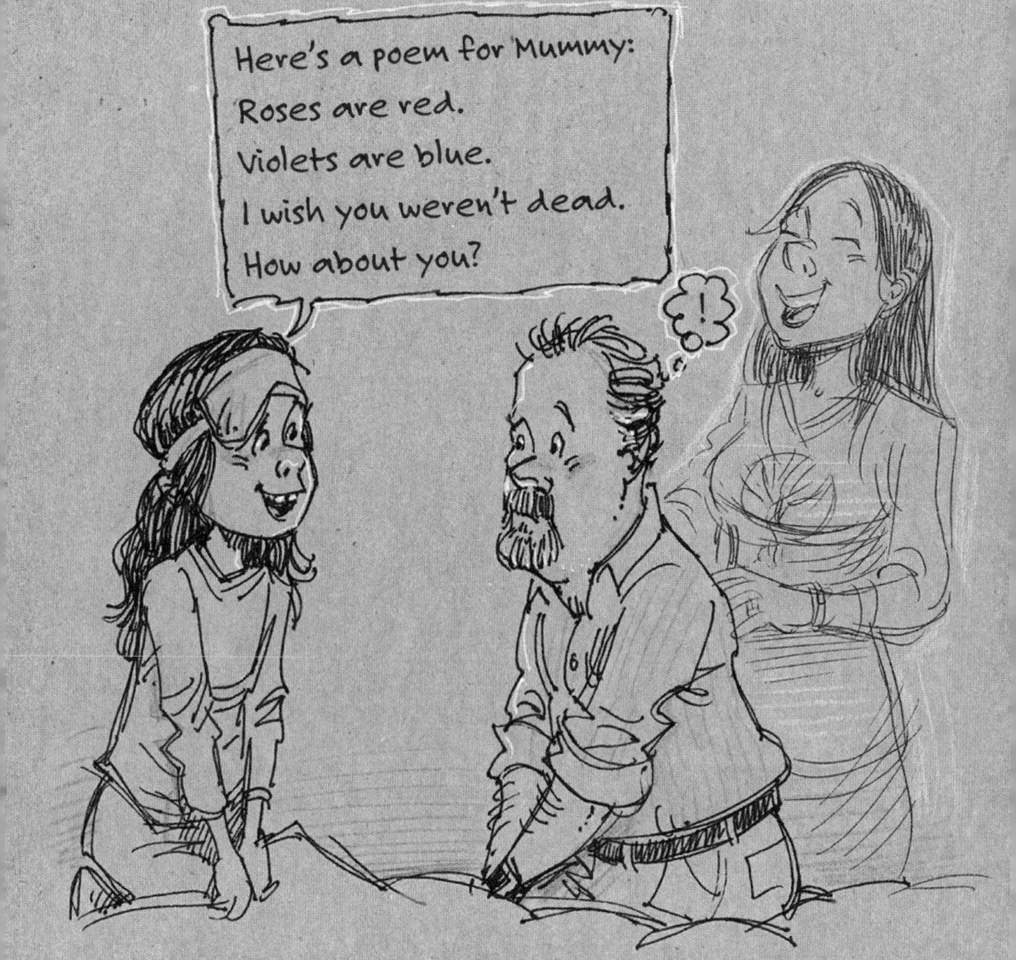
Here's a poem for Mummy:
Roses are red.
Violets are blue.
I wish you weren't dead.
How about you?
!

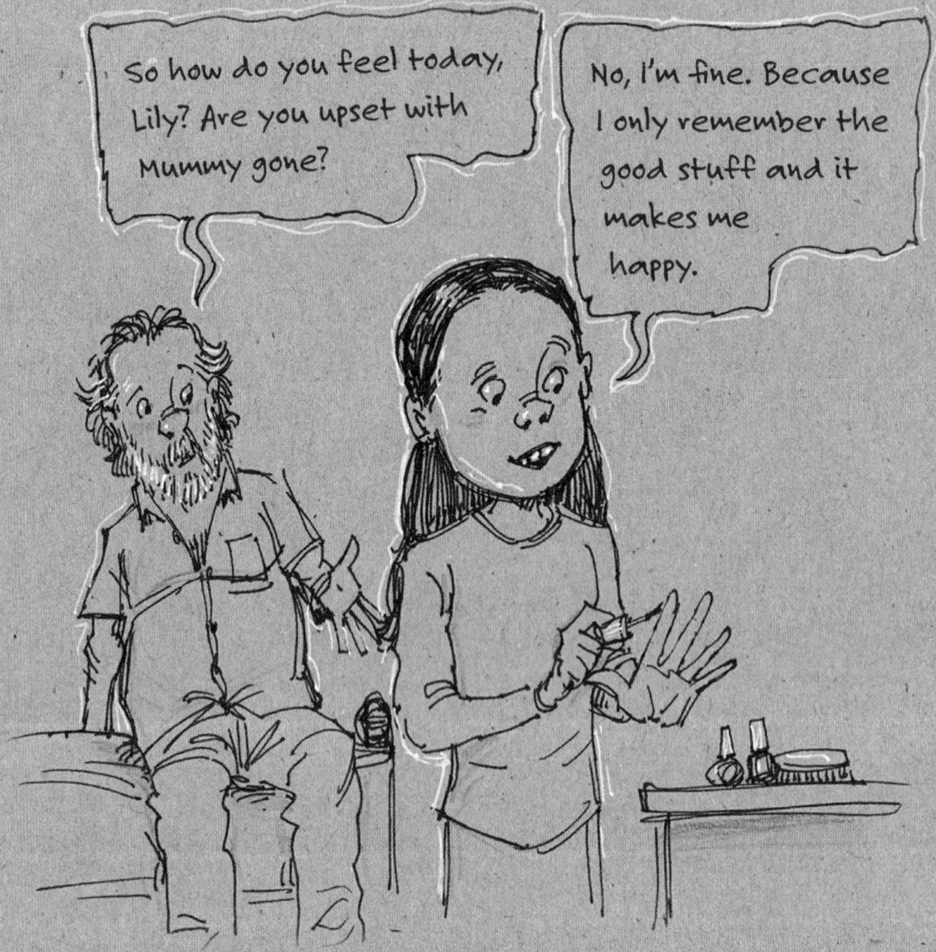
So how do you feel today, Lily? Are you upset with Mummy gone?
No, I'm fine. Because I only remember the good stuff and it makes me happy.

Mothering Sunday.

And Ben was . . . Ben

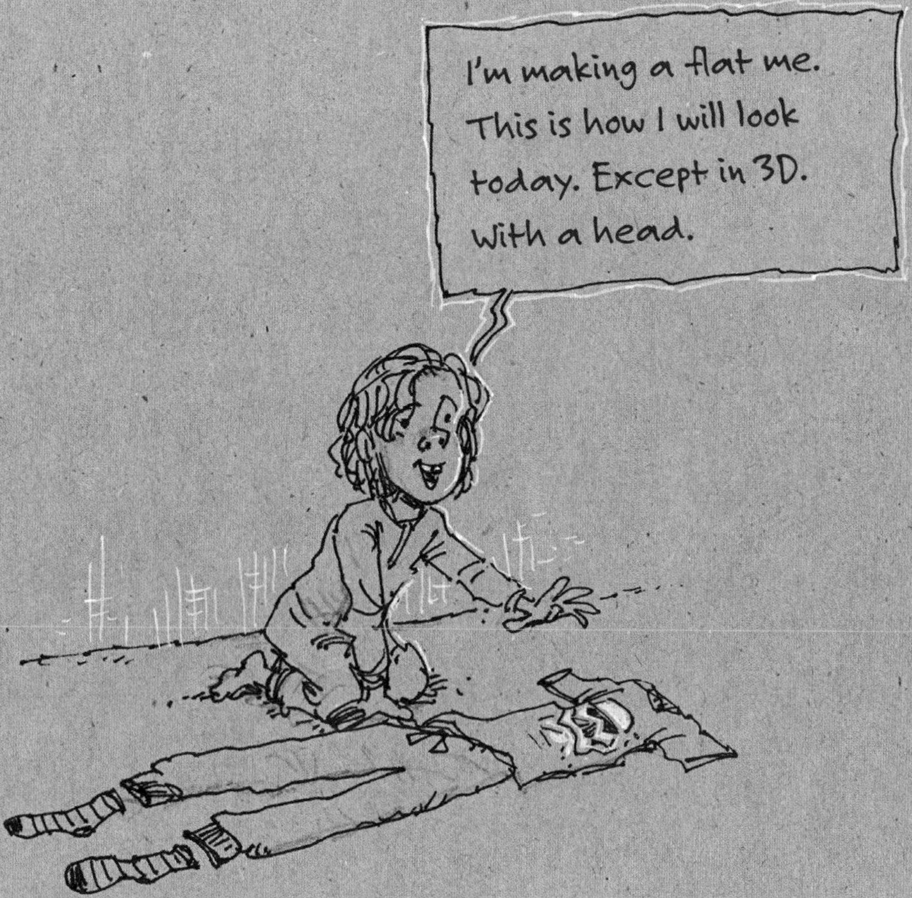
I'm making a flat me. This is how I will look today. Except in 3D. With a head.

Six months on and I was still working on some things.

Sometimes it felt as if the kids were looking after *me* ...

*Feeling crap – having a bath and getting read to by
Ben from his magazine (all about poo).*

. . . and each other.

Hard to know where one ends and the other begins . . .
literally and metaphorically!

The grief felt different from one day to the next. Some days memories would invade without a moment's notice and I'd feel angry at the unfairness of it all.

Letting the dog out into the garden, the smell of cut grass and woodsmoke reminded me of beautiful summer evenings past, when we would sit hand in hand as the sun set. Precious memories of a life before the pain.

Other days, when the sun shone and plans were made, my grief would feel like a strange comfort, a familiar feeling that reminded me of a perfect love.

I could feel hopeful for the future . . .

...and hopeless again in an instant.

When you watch the perfect final episode of a favourite TV show you used to watch together, and it dawns on you she will never see it.

I came to realise how important it was to spend time doing things that brought joy, like talking with good friends who understood what I needed, whether that was help with the kids, a laugh and a chat or simply to share an evening in front of the TV and not be alone...

. . . even if I wasn't always the best company.

I returned to my favourite hobbies . . .

*I can always count on Shakespeare to lift me up
when I need it.*

... some of which run in the family, luckily.

It felt good for all of us to return to old habits.

Such a treat to be watching a play together and
sharing this glorious, healing laughter.

It was particularly important to me to keep up some traditions Joy and I had started, like our annual garden party close to her birthday.

It felt as though you were there, just out of sight, around the corner. You were so loved.

Cherishing old habits helped make embracing new traditions without Joy easier.

The kids spent the afternoon with Gran'ma and came back with home-made cheese scones. This is going to be a regular thing. Go, Gran'ma!

Mud run with the kids...I could practically hear you laughing.

However, there were some coping mechanisms I started to regret!

Whoops! I may have inadvertently eaten a whole tub of ice cream tonight.

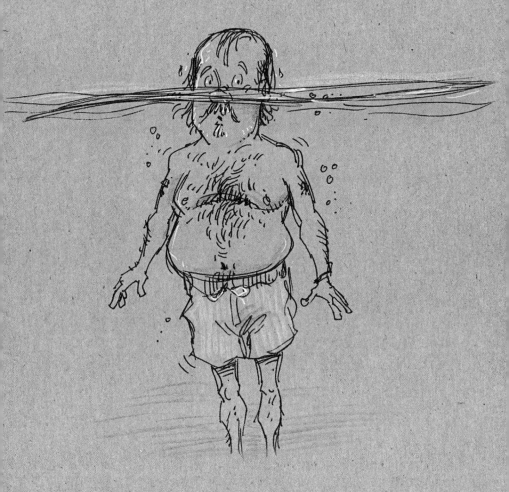

Went swimming and literally bobbed like a cork...
Think I need to lose a bit of weight!

So, eight months in, I decided it was time to take matters in hand and try to get fit again…

...even if I was a bit rusty.

Only one thought crossing my mind...

The grief was a constant learning process. The kids taught me so much – the way they lived in the present while acknowledging the past . . .

Watching Pixar's 'Coco'.

. . . their brutal honesty . . .

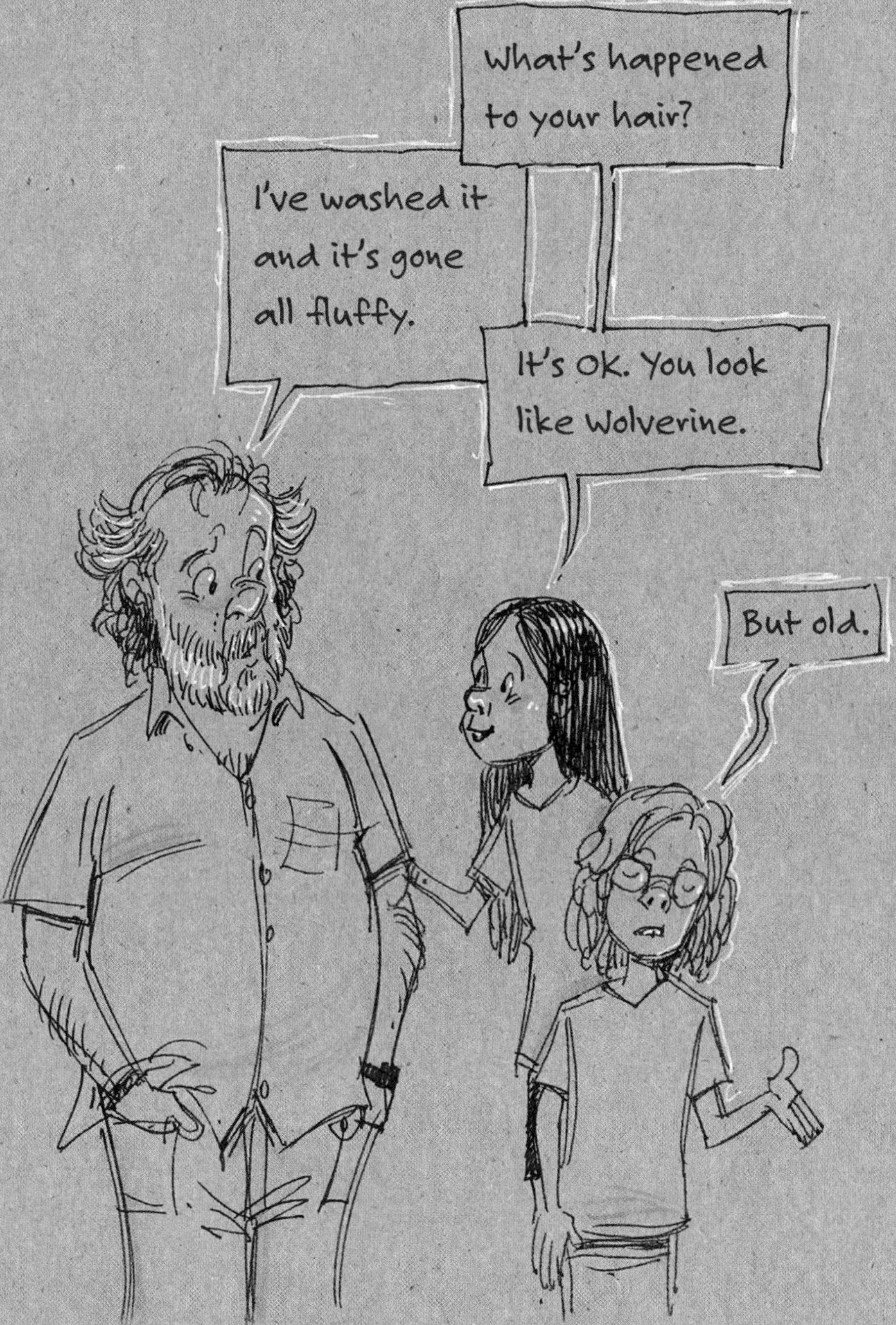
What's happened to your hair?
I've washed it and it's gone all fluffy.
It's OK. You look like Wolverine.
But old.

...and the simplicity of their world view.

Mind you, sometimes it could all get a bit much!

When it came round to going on holiday for the first time without Joy, I was dreading it …

... but when we were there, I could imagine her with me and it was strangely comforting.

I hear you in their laughs and see you in their eyes. I miss you in my arms.

It was a wonderful week.

Ben: Dad, I'm going to make your belly button talk.
Lily: I'll make your boobs the eyes.

Fatherhood is a dignity-free zone.

Dad jobs: underwater double piggybacks.

Trying to get the kids to bed on the last night of the holiday...

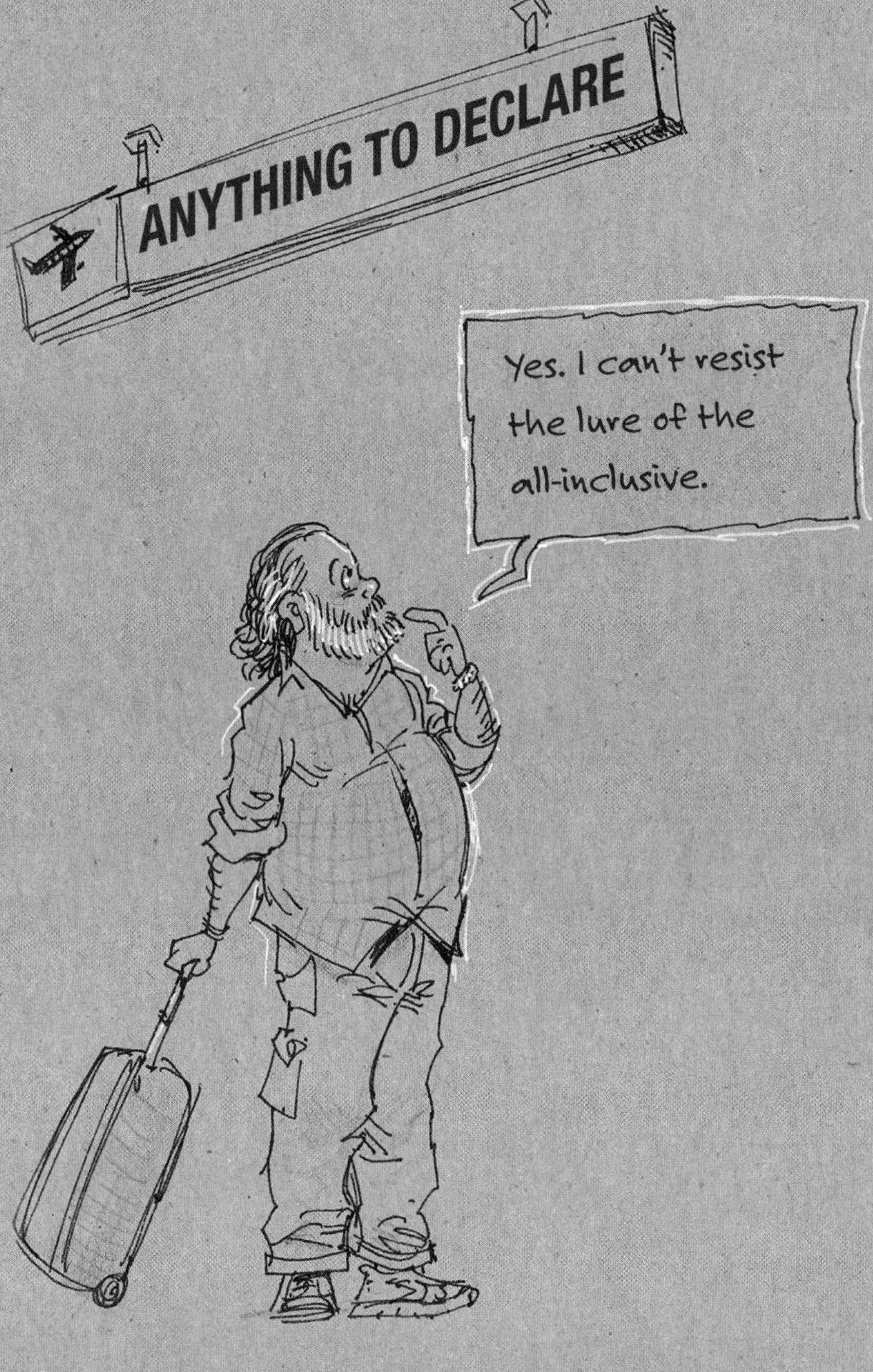
ANYTHING TO DECLARE
Yes. I can't resist the lure of the all-inclusive.

But when we came back and I went shopping for three instead of four, the grief came back with a vengeance. The roller coaster was far from over.

My relationship with grief had been constantly evolving.

One month:
oppressor.

Six months:
shadow.

Ten months:
companion.

We were all on our journeys, coming to terms with Joy's absence in our own ways.

On your forty-second birthday we scattered some of your ashes in a beautiful, tangled spot at the end of the garden, marked by a stone. It is rough and unpolished. You would love it.

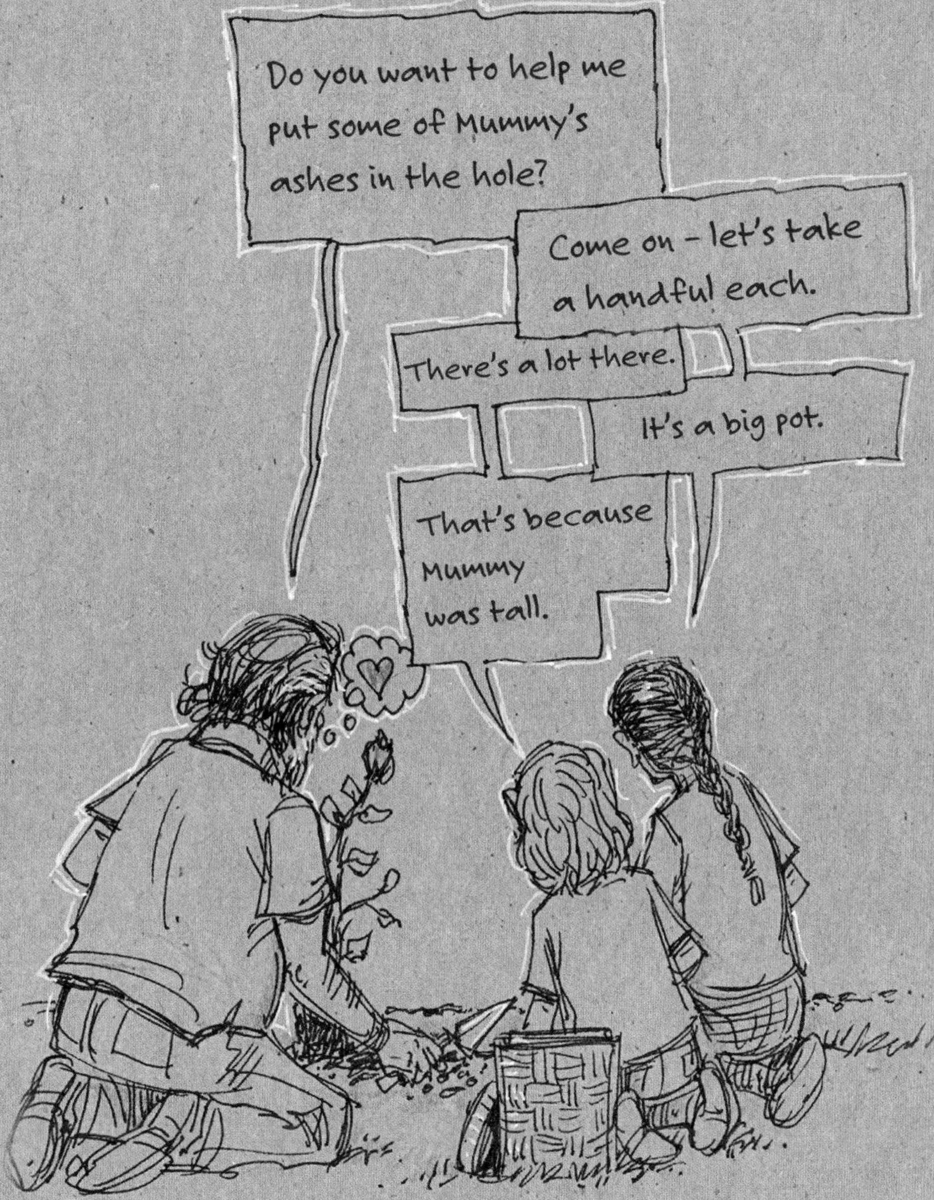
Do you want to help me put some of Mummy's ashes in the hole?
Come on – let's take a handful each.
There's a lot there.
It's a big pot.
That's because Mummy was tall.

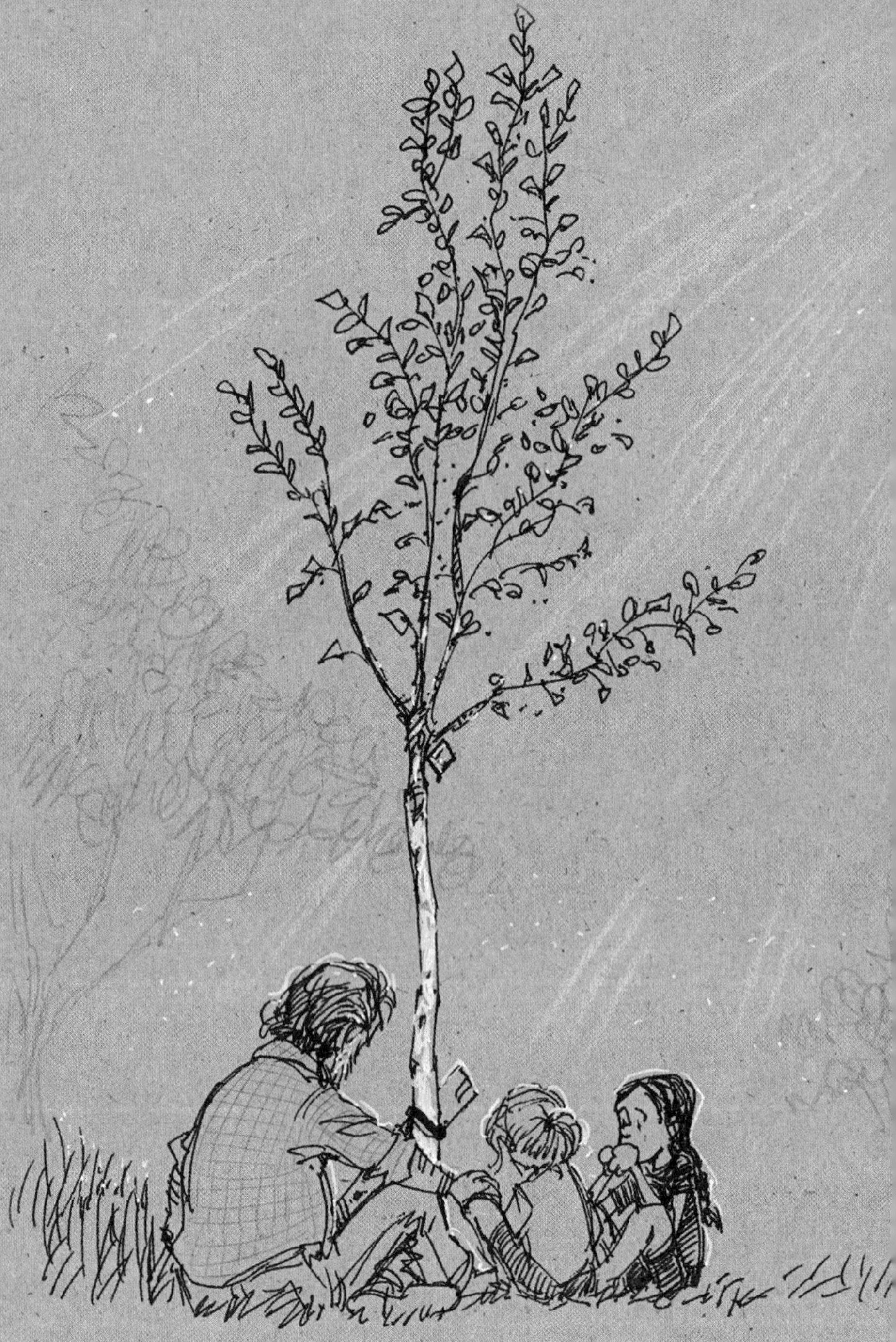

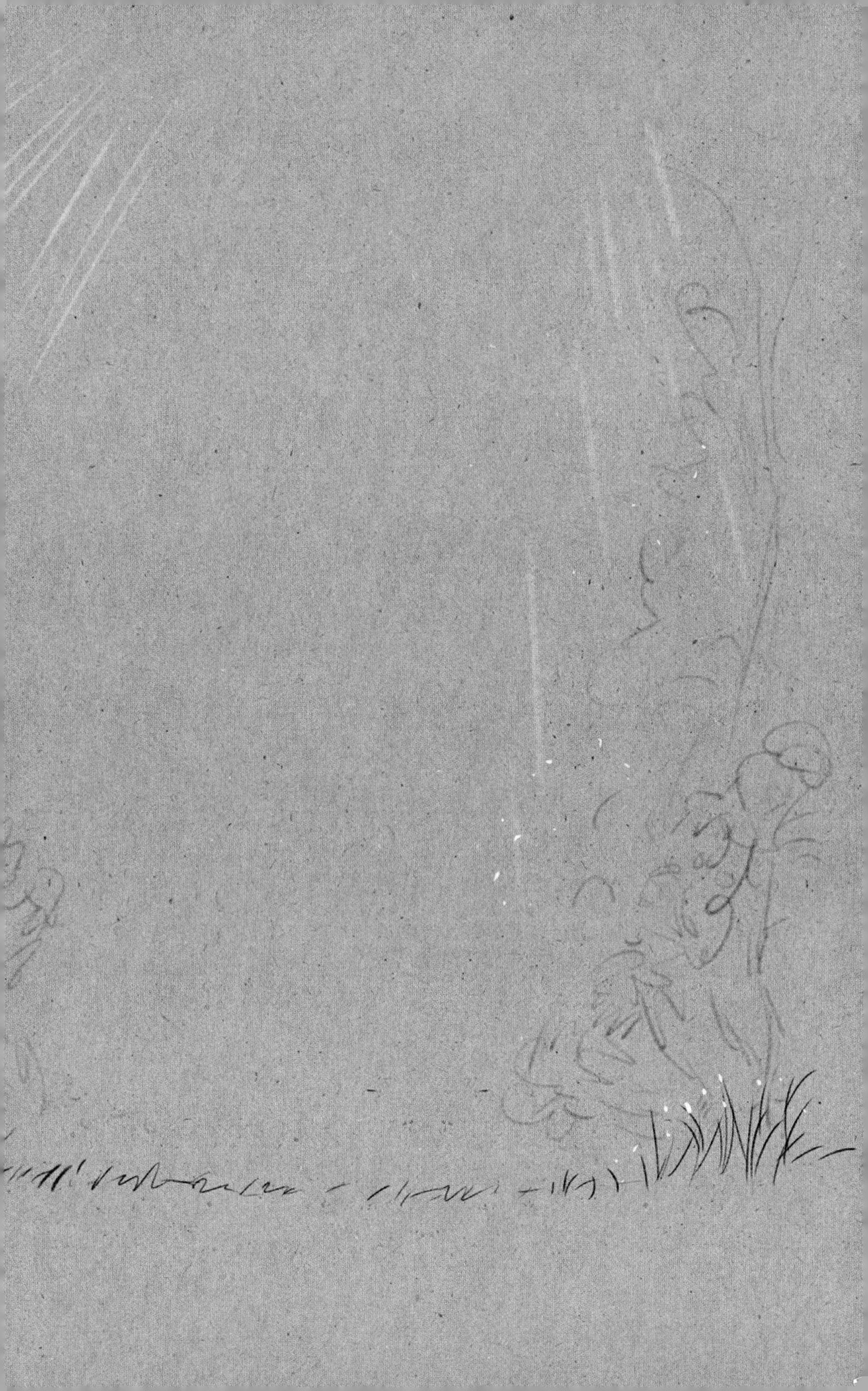

Juggling work and parenting on my own often felt completely overwhelming. I kept telling myself things would get better, but it was still difficult.

Sometimes the smallest things would catch me off guard.

I had a good day. Then, just as I got home, our wedding song came on the car radio and I could barely get my key in the door.

But I was also learning that the simplest of things could give me great comfort, too, and to cherish these moments.

I always feel you with me when I am surrounded by trees. Today was a good day.

Coming home late, hoping the kids have gone to sleep but being secretly delighted that they are still awake so I get one more cuddle.

I marvelled at how the kids had been processing the experience, and I was very glad they could share their thoughts with me...

... even if sometimes they lacked a little tact!

Despite appearances . . .

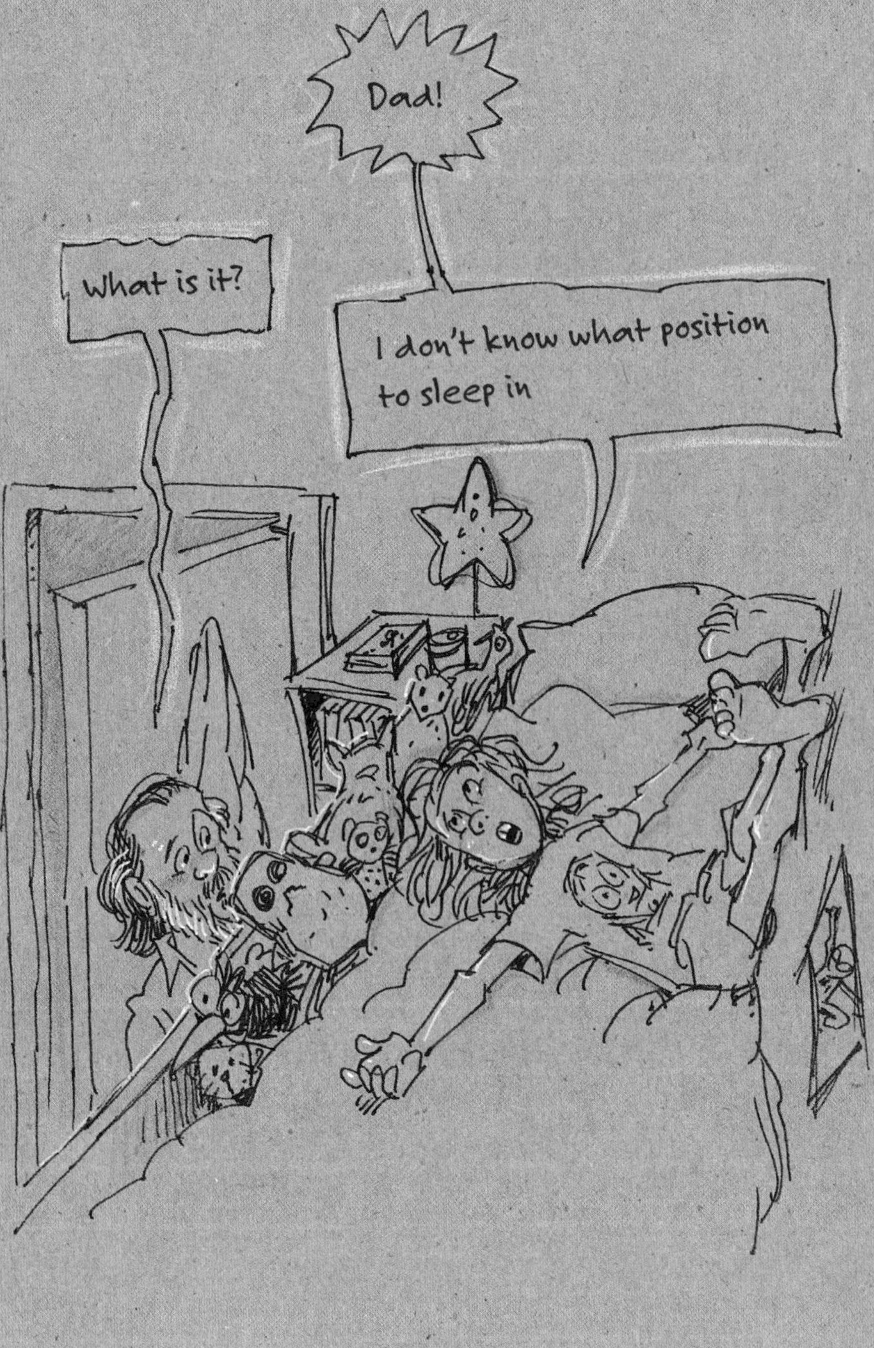
Dad!
What is it?
I don't know what position to sleep in

... sometimes the best wisdom would come from the most unexpected of sources.

The summer holidays came to an end and we went through the yearly ritual of sorting out old clothes and buying new ones. It felt like healing.

That's it. School bags packed and in the hall ready
for the morning. Summer over and a new school year
begins. We did it. We made it through the long holiday.
Ticking off those challenges one at a time…

The wheel turned – round and round, on and on – and suddenly it was a year since Joy had died.

I visited your tree today without crying... Told you everything that's going on. I know you would be pleased. Still wish I didn't have to do it though.

So much had changed in that year.

Did you just grow up four years overnight?

Every little cough and sniffle put me on edge.

I know they're fine, but I worry...

I liked to think that, even though the grief was still there, so was Joy – always at my shoulder, a part of everything still.

*I love that I can come and sit at the end of the garden
and talk to you about my plans.*

While some things had remained the same...

I have the whole bed to myself, yet still sleep on 'my side'.

...I noticed that my attempts to look after myself were paying off, and I was making good progress.

Put my trousers on and they felt funny. Then I realised...the belt was a notch tighter!

I felt able to make important decisions that I couldn't have imagined a year earlier.

Last night I moved my wedding ring to the other hand. A symbol of our love, always remembered, but it is time to move forward. You are gone and I can't change that. I will always love you, but I need to acknowledge that life has changed. I know you understand – you always knew best.

Finally facing a weekend of decluttering and reorganising. The physical process is very symbolic of the mental one.

I noticed that my relationship with Lily and Ben had changed too – we had become more of a team.

Well, not always . . .

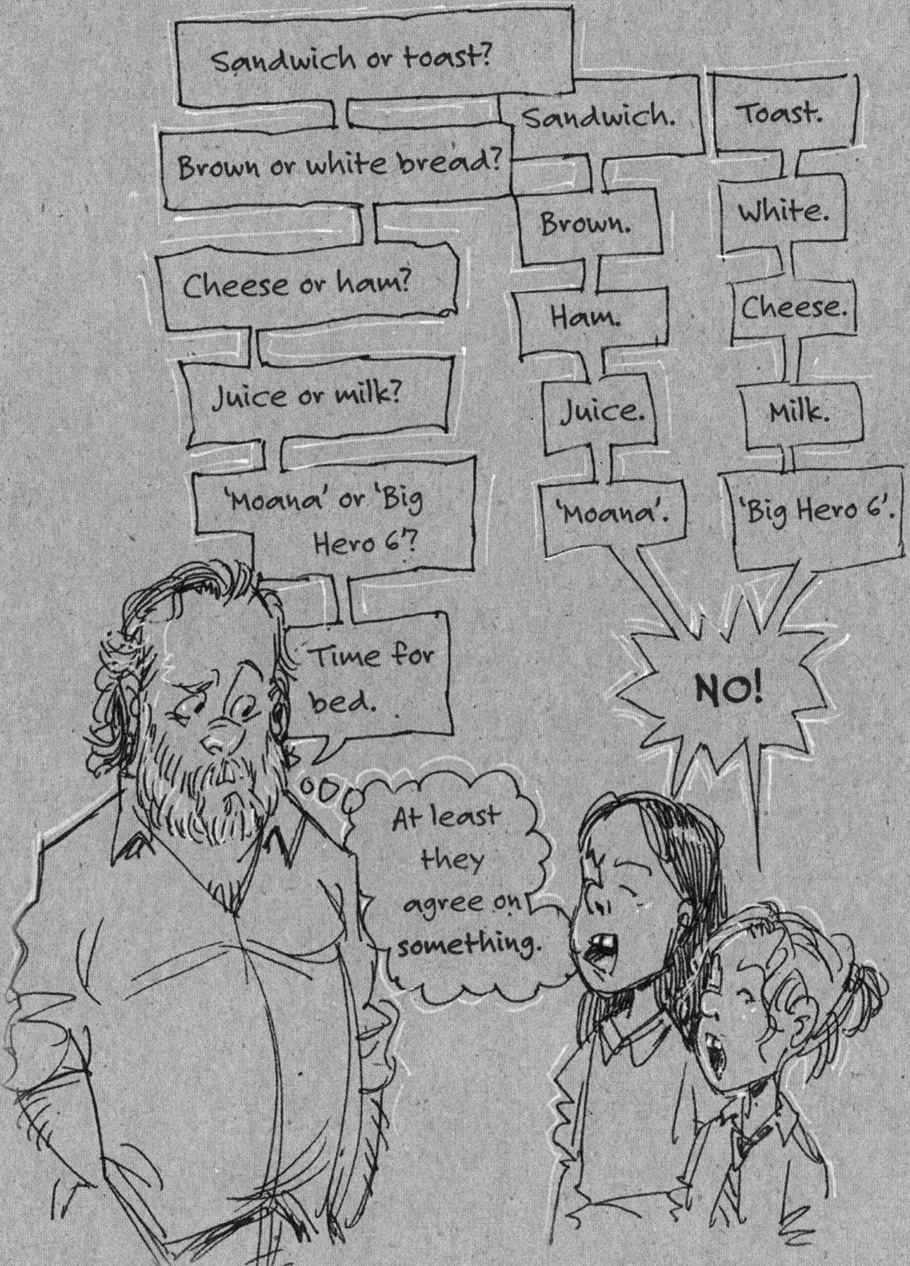
Sandwich or toast?
Sandwich.
Toast.
Brown or white bread?
Brown.
White.
Cheese or ham?
Ham.
Cheese.
Juice or milk?
Juice.
Milk.
'Moana' or 'Big Hero 6'?
'Moana'.
'Big Hero 6'.
Time for bed.
NO!
At least they agree on something.

It was sometimes easy to forget that they were still very young, despite seeming so grown up.

*Worst feeling:
Getting really angry
when they just
won't behave.*

*Best feeling:
Making-up
cuddles.*

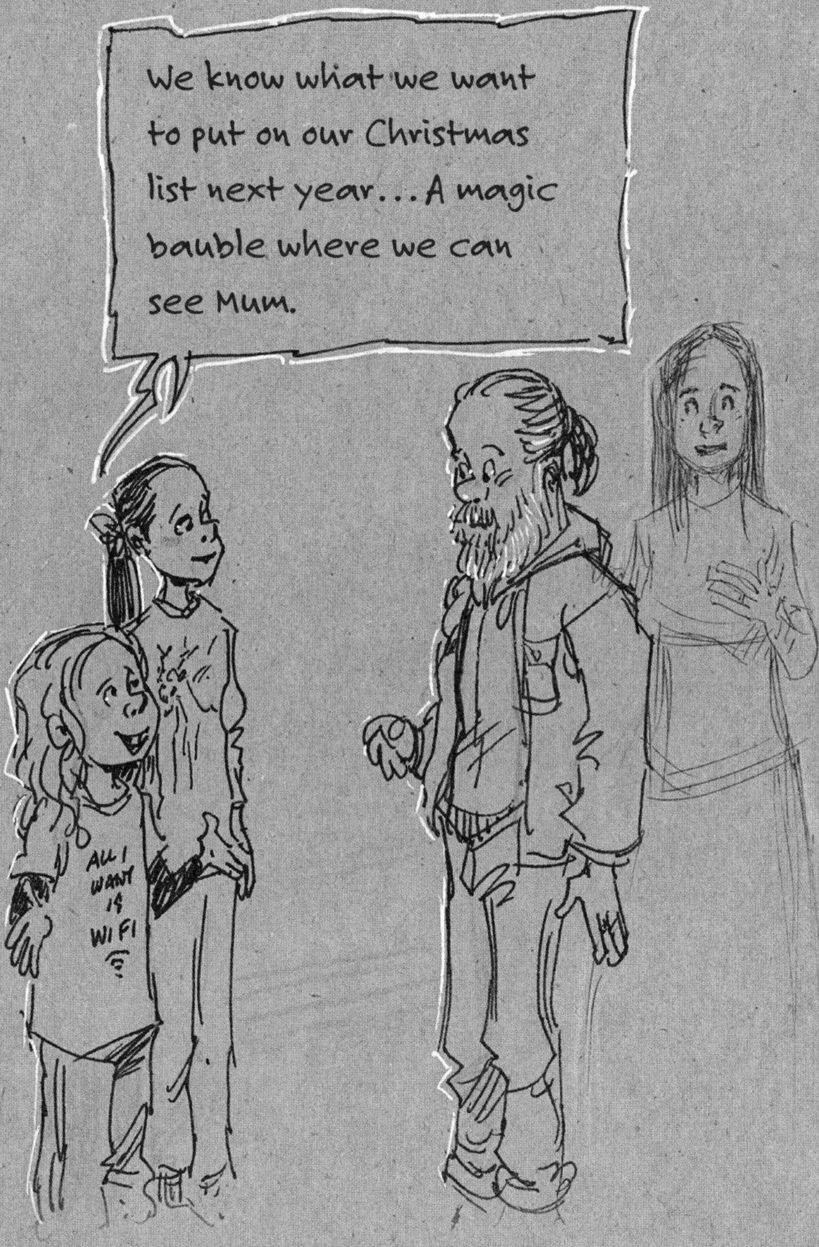
We know what we want to put on our Christmas list next year... A magic bauble where we can see Mum.
ALL I WANT IS WIFI

Being both Mum and Dad wasn't easy.

I always think, 'What would you say?'

The balance had changed in the house, especially after our dog died as well, and that was something I couldn't fix.

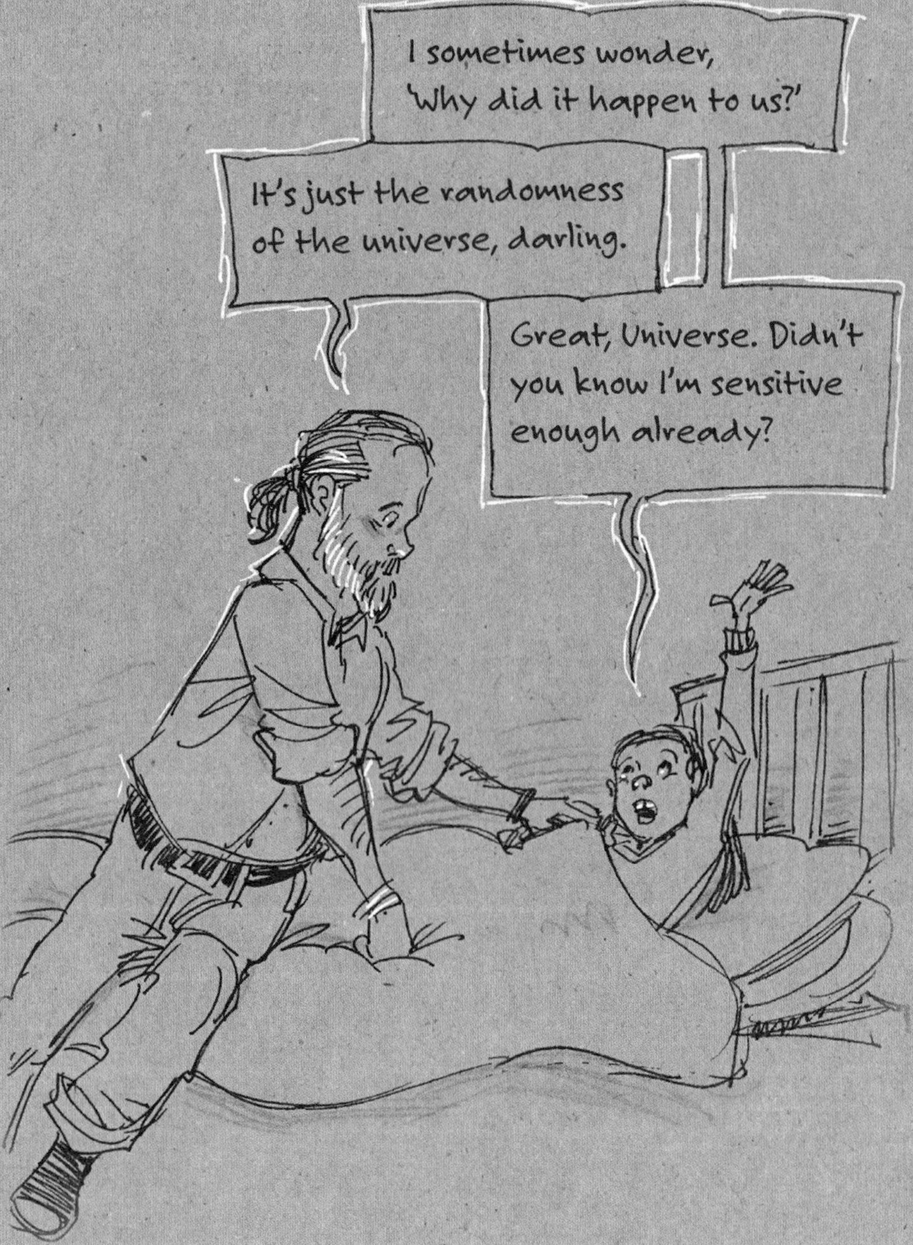
I sometimes wonder, 'Why did it happen to us?'
It's just the randomness of the universe, darling.
Great, Universe. Didn't you know I'm sensitive enough already?

Sometimes just being there is enough.

*The definition of love and trust: submitting to
'Salon Lily' when your ten-year-old decides she
wants to tidy your eyebrows.*

Today it was the turn of 'Salon Daddy'.

They were still healing too. Communication was very important. We always talked about Joy and kept her part of our everyday life.

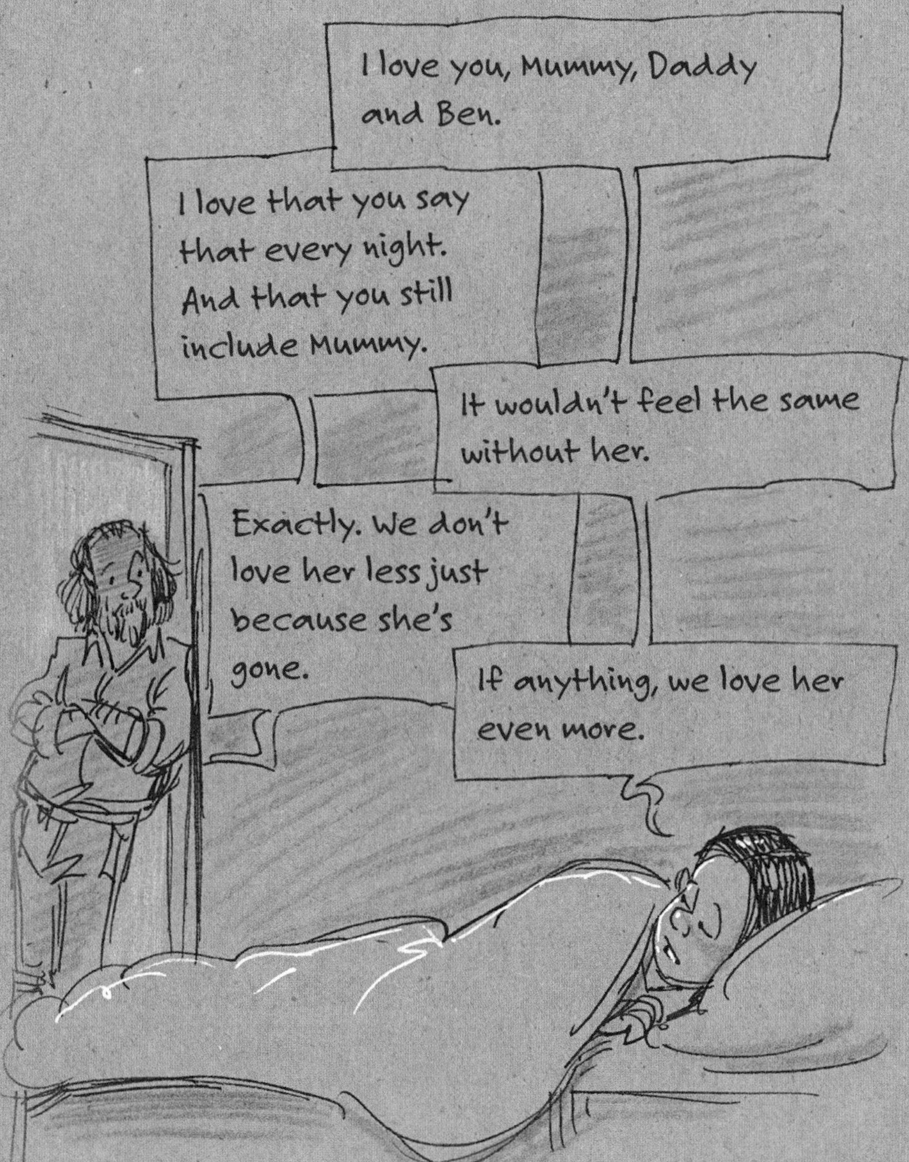
I love you, Mummy, Daddy and Ben.
I love that you say that every night. And that you still include Mummy.
It wouldn't feel the same without her.
Exactly. We don't love her less just because she's gone.
If anything, we love her even more.

Lily and Ben had become my main companions.

Sitting opposite the kids at lunch, I was suddenly overwhelmed by the love I have for them. Since Joy's death they have become my best friends.

Not the life I expected to be living, but one I take huge pride in.

They were always there to make me smile...

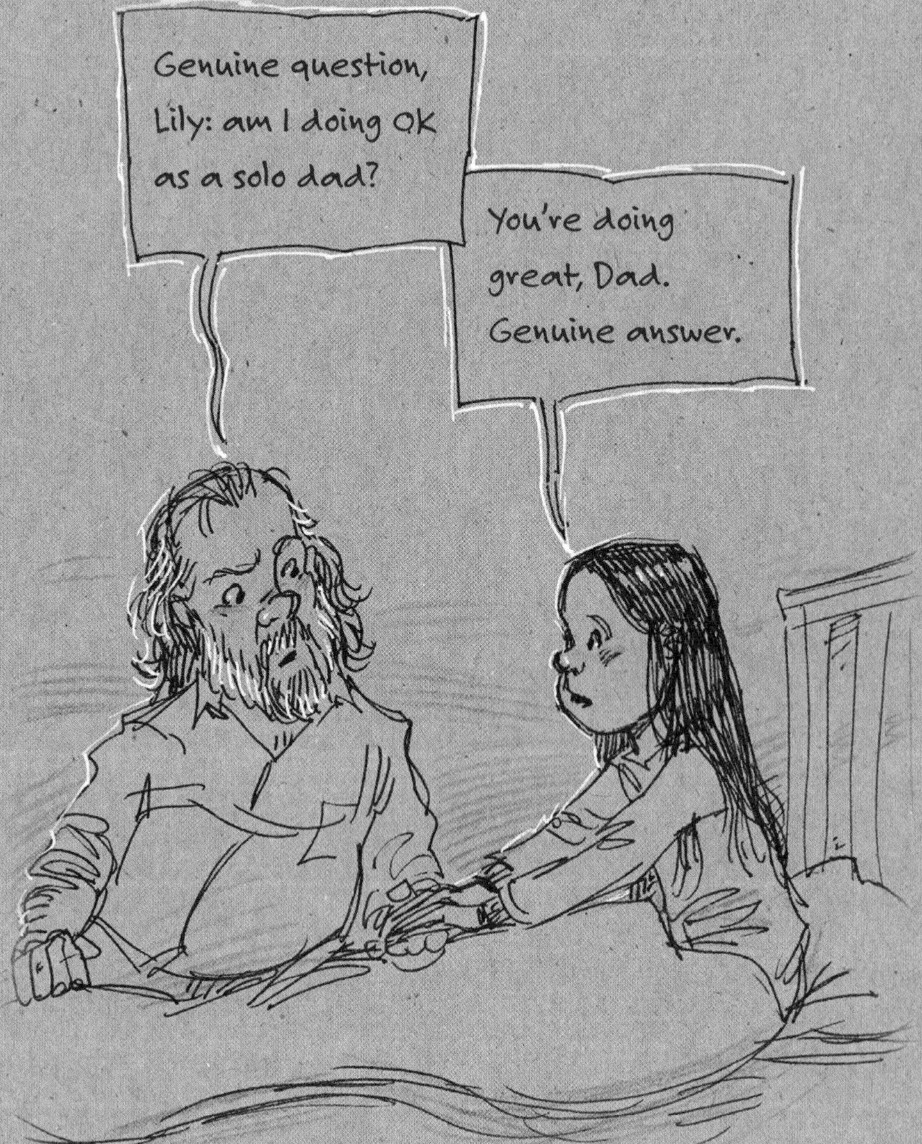
Genuine question, Lily: am I doing OK as a solo dad?
You're doing great, Dad. Genuine answer.

...and sometimes to take my breath away.

We were figuring this out together.

Mother's Day visit to Joy's tree. We left our messages, then while I stood and remembered times past the kids climbed and played nearby.

A snapshot of our 'new normal'.

Just as I got used to our new way of life, I'd still have days where it seemed unbelievable.

One of those days that found me sitting in the car for ten minutes after the school run, shaking my head in disbelief that it's been a year and a half since our lives changed so dramatically – and it isn't just some stupid dream.

Yet I noticed that I was starting to approach my grief with love and gratitude more than sadness.

Going through an old rucksack today, I unexpectedly came across one of your scarves. It still smelled of you. This didn't prompt tears, however, but rather a smile. I'm so glad that you were a part of my life.

After eighteen months, the grief informed my life but didn't define it.

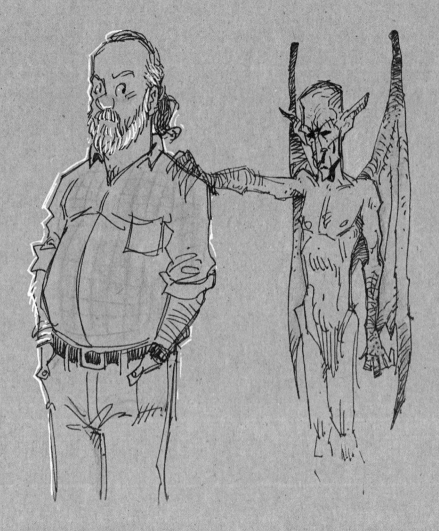

The Grief Demon takes a back seat these days, but never fully goes away. A gentle hand on my shoulder, reminding me he's still there. Sometimes I can brush him off, and other times I invite him in. It's mostly my choice now. Mostly.

It was time to take stock of my life. Yes, I am a widower but I'm also a director...

Buzzing after a terrific evening of auditions for A Comedy of Errors. *My boy Bill never lets me down!*

...a keen cook...

... and an exercise enthusiast (if not always a successful one).

A hair model . . .

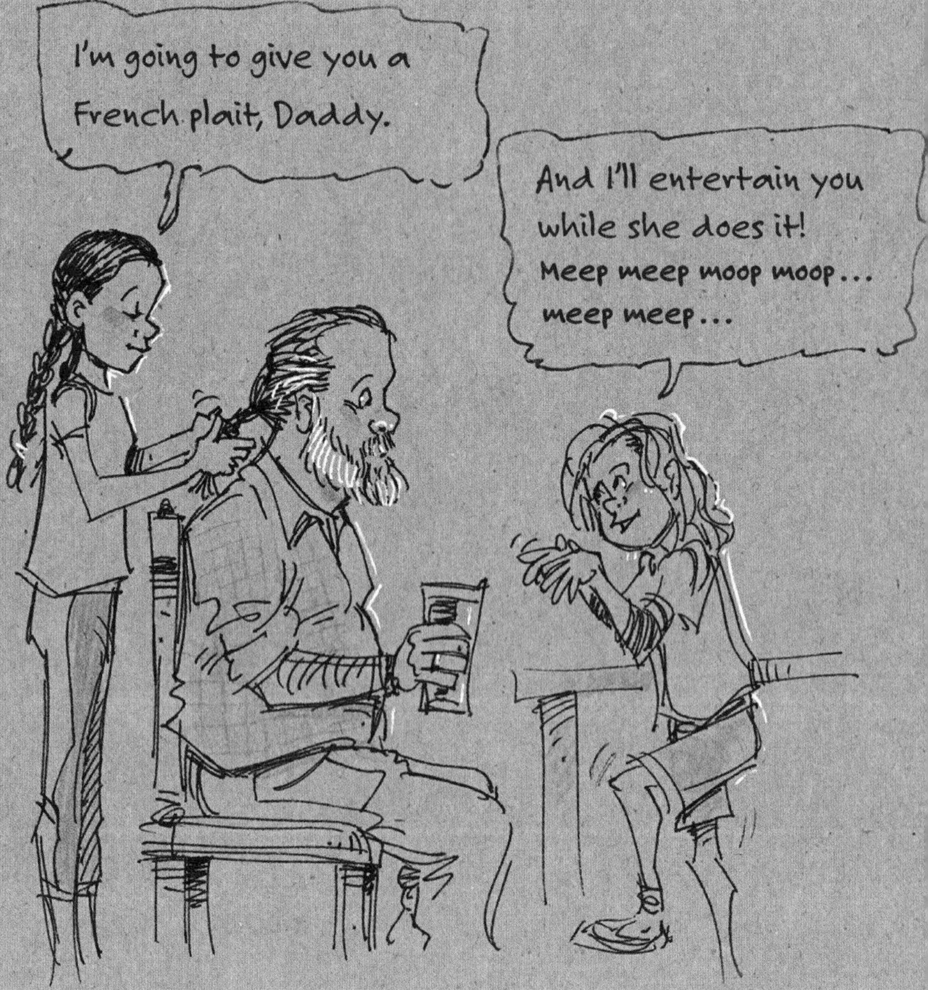
I'm going to give you a French plait, Daddy.
And I'll entertain you while she does it! Meep meep moop moop . . . meep meep . . .

... a bringer of food ...

How it feels feeding the kids.

. . . a proud father . . .

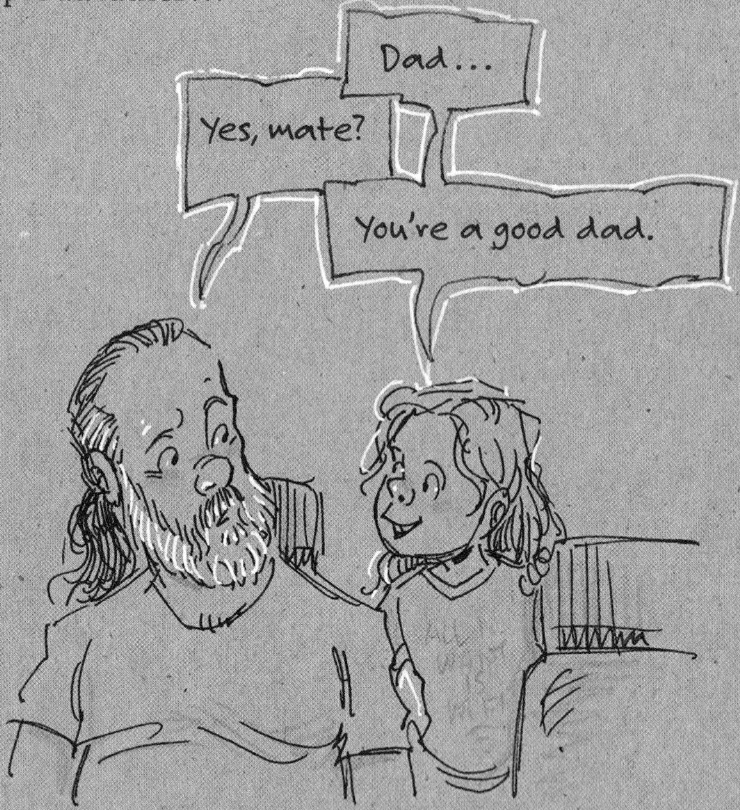
Dad...
Yes, mate?
You're a good dad.

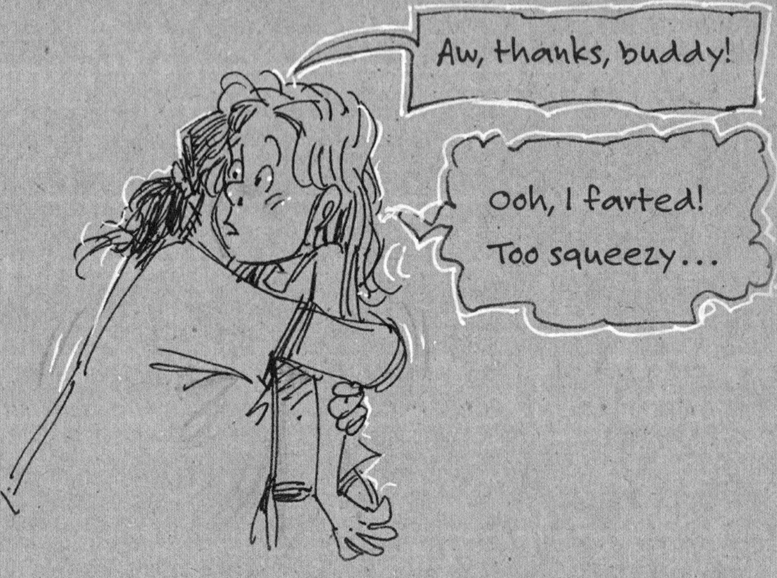
Aw, thanks, buddy!
Ooh, I farted!
Too squeezy...

...and a man privileged to have known a love like Joy's.

Came across a couple of photos of you that prompted a visit from the Grief Demon. But it was a welcome one. Damn, I was so lucky.

I was learning to accept that there would always be days when I would need to pause for a moment ...

I bought new bedding at the weekend. It just dawned on me that these are the first sheets on our bed that you never slept in. There were a few tears to acknowledge that.

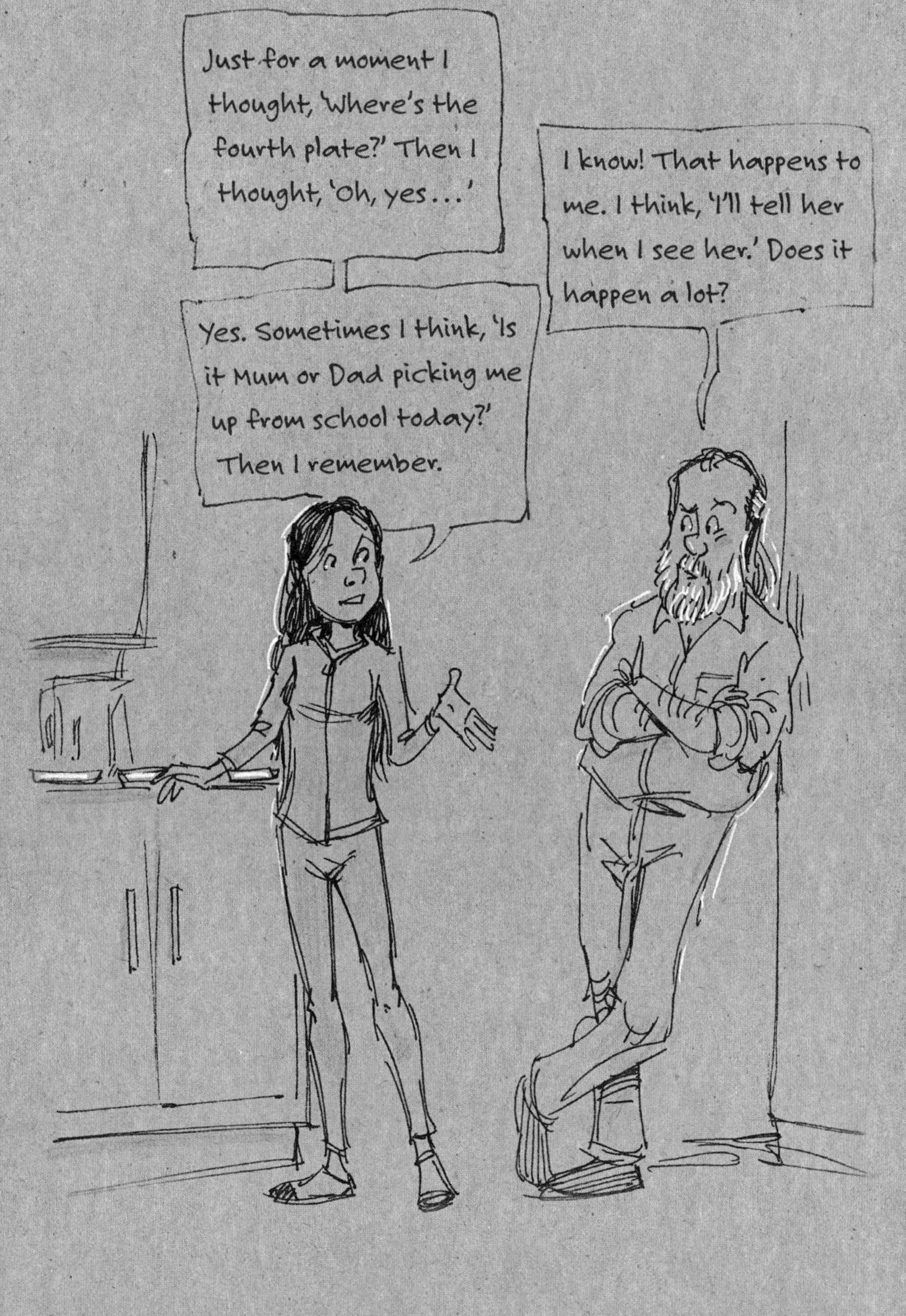
Just for a moment I thought, 'Where's the fourth plate?' Then I thought, 'Oh, yes . . .'
Yes. Sometimes I think, 'Is it Mum or Dad picking me up from school today?' Then I remember.
I know! That happens to me. I think, 'I'll tell her when I see her.' Does it happen a lot?

'...that sometimes it would all feel too much.

Today was one of those
'How on earth can you be gone?' days.

*I know we were just making it up as we went along,
but it was so much easier when we were making it up
together. Still, I always think, 'Would you approve?'
And if the answer is 'yes', I can't be too wrong.*

But slowly things were changing without me even realising it.

I have finally discovered the delights of the 'diagonal'.

I was casually pulling up weeds around Joy's stone
when it struck me that this is now just another thing I
do, like cooking dinner or cutting the grass. I suppose
this is acceptance. Certainly I was at peace doing it.
The love goes on while the pain recedes …

The Grief Demon and I were able to co-exist in an uneasy truce. But it was now on my terms...

...unlike the bathroom rota.

'Big school' brought new challenges for Lily that she handled remarkably well.

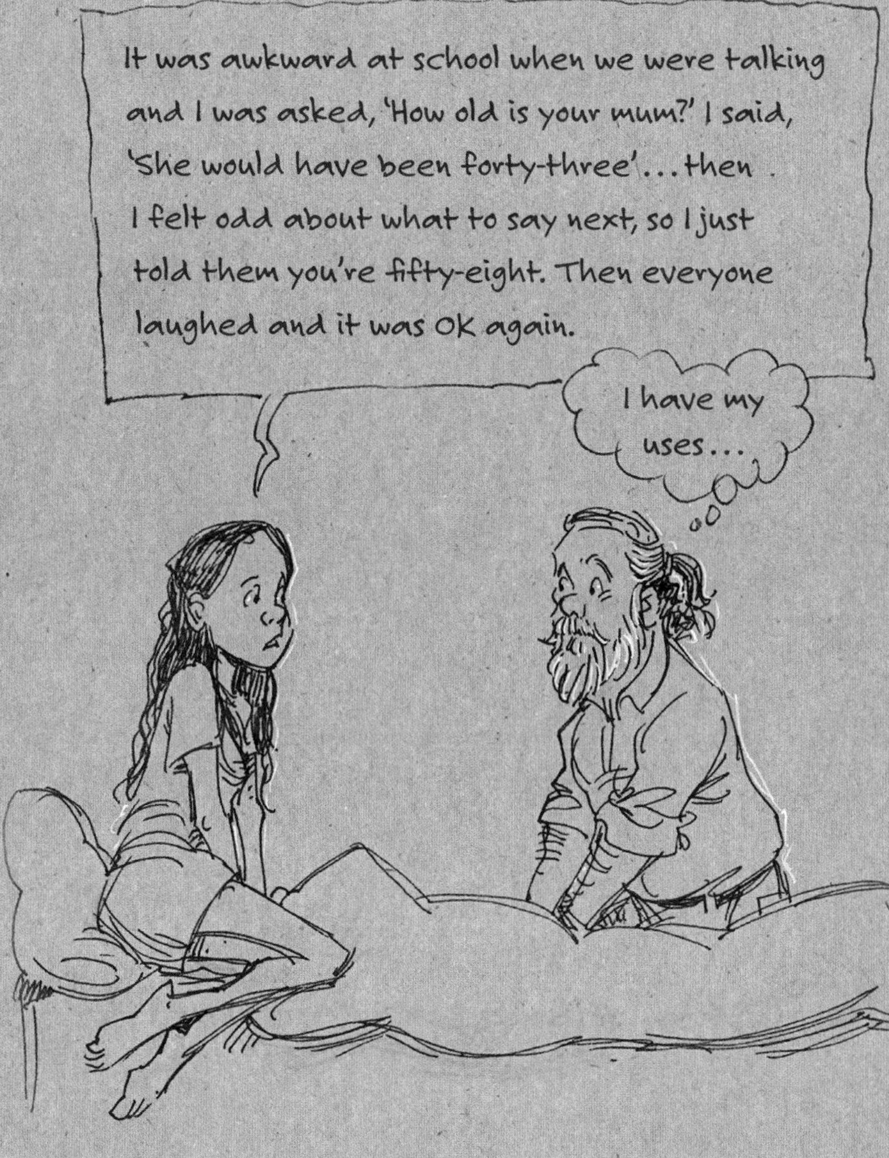
It was awkward at school when we were talking and I was asked, 'How old is your mum?' I said, 'She would have been forty-three'... then I felt odd about what to say next, so I just told them you're fifty-eight. Then everyone laughed and it was OK again.
I have my uses...

Although we were moving forward, the past could also bring its own comforts. It was important to treasure those memories.

One of the great advantages of keeping these doodle diaries is that when Lily can't sleep, because her mind is full of big thoughts, she loves to come downstairs and look through them.

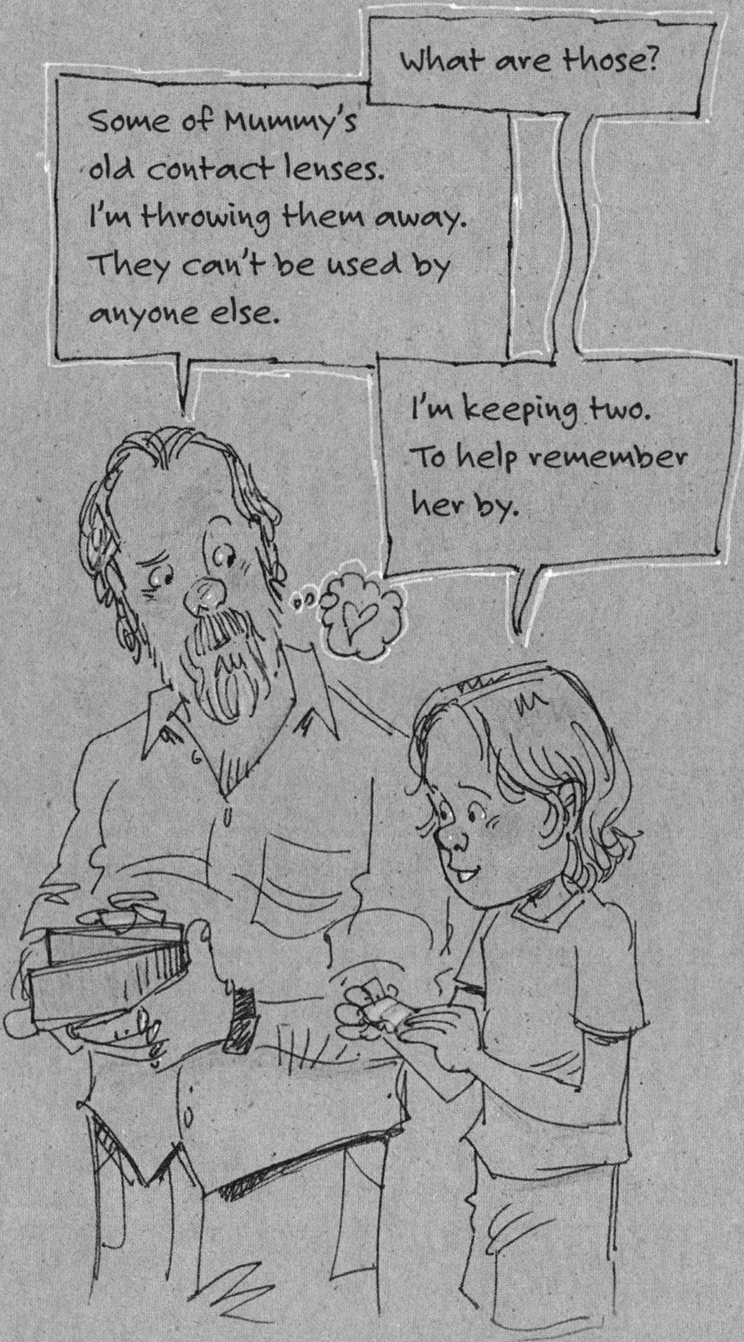
What are those?
Some of Mummy's old contact lenses. I'm throwing them away. They can't be used by anyone else.
I'm keeping two. To help remember her by.

Two years on and day to day I was in a positive place, but there were still those reminders of what was lost that I couldn't avoid.

Despite everything, there is one thing I really find hard. That empty bed. I still catch myself putting off going upstairs for as long as I can.

Sometimes it seems so long I can barely remember how it felt to have you there…Other times it's as though you have just popped out to the shops.

The bizarre dual timeline of grief.

Grief takes many forms and manifests in a multitude of ways. Sitting in a restaurant, looking around at the other families, I felt a huge sense of loss. It's so sad for my kids that they have just me and not Mummy. We are incredibly close but there is such a vital piece missing.

Christmas was always an emotional time of year, when Joy's absence was particularly noticeable.

The day after Boxing Day, hereafter to be called 'Piles Day'.

Piles of memories. Piles of wrapping paper.
Piles of laundry. Piles of cheese. Piles of presents.

Christmas is all packed away back in the loft. The kids have gone to bed. Suddenly everything is back to 'normal'. And it feels very empty…very lonely. So, I put on a well-loved DVD and let it wash over me, imagining you beside me.

After the euphoria of the last few days, this morning I
was hit by a post-Christmas slump, just wanting to do
nothing. Empty. The feeling passed, but left its shadow…

Yet, three Christmases on, it was easier to bounce back than before.

After yesterday's contemplative melancholy, today you were right there, riding that grief roller coaster with me.

I came to realise that the positive days now outnumbered the negative. Things that used to upset me could now bring me comfort.

Sorting through the last few years' photo albums today... hundreds of photos of you. You felt so close: bewildering to think you weren't just in the next room. But, above all, it made me smile. We had a great time together, didn't we?

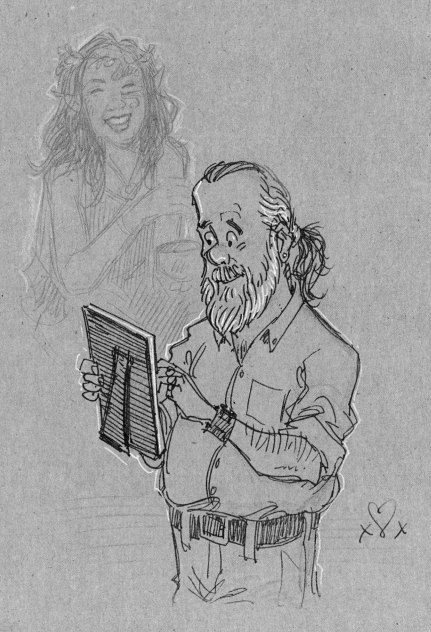

One photo – a beautiful photo of you laughing – has put your smile and your laugh in my head for the last couple of days. And it has made me smile too. Not a bittersweet smile, but one of genuine delight that I was lucky enough to have you in my life.

I thought back on the years leading up to this point, and to those who helped me get here...

Kindness, in all its forms, has made our lives better. From school pick-ups to sleepovers, the gift of a book mentioned in passing – even simple messages have all made such a difference.

... especially my kids, whose energy and enthusiasm for life never fails to inspire me.

Suddenly it was another New Year, and the Grief Demon was no longer on my back or one step behind.

He's still here, in the room – not welcome, but tolerated. Sometimes he takes me by surprise. Sometimes I invite him closer. Our relationship constantly evolves, but it is a power struggle that I'm slowly winning.

And I find myself approaching life with a new purpose.

Gave a talk today about child bereavement. I would give the world not to be in this position, but…

…I am. And it's an honour and a privilege to do so. To be able to communicate to others about grief management makes Joy's death less pointless.

*I love that I have a place in the garden where I can go
to feel close to you, to light a candle or lay wild flowers
on special days – although I don't need to go there to
feel you. You are always with me.*

When we married, we made a promise that we would
be together until parted by death. We could never
have predicted that our parting would come so soon.
I love you as much today as I did then.

That love sustains me still, guiding me, inspiring me. It
makes me strive to be a better person, a better friend,
a better father…

… and I move forward with hope. Hope for my future, hope for my kids – and I know, if I honour your memory, I have hope of finding joy.

Help and advice

I don't claim to be any kind of an expert in coping with grief but I thought it might help if I listed a few things I have noticed or found useful in going through this myself. Everyone's journey is different but sometimes it helps to have a guide who knows the path.

- Talking is good. Don't bottle up those feelings.

- Your friends have lost the person as well and sometimes *they* may want to talk. Let them.

- If friends ask you if you need help, accept their kindness. If they didn't mean it, they wouldn't offer.

- My friends set up a WhatsApp group so if I needed help I could send a message and someone would be able to come forward. Having a support network is vital.

- Social media can be a comforting place. I am lucky that these days I have a large following but in the early days, before the doodles took off, it was just a few friends and family. Sometimes late at night if I was feeling sad I would go live – there was always someone there who would comment and let you know you were not alone.

- I've developed several firm friendships by following other grieving people online. There is nothing like speaking with someone else who is going through a similar pain.

- It's OK to laugh still – life DOES go on.

Illness, grief and bereavement

UK Sepsis Trust works to fight sepsis, stop preventable deaths and support those affected by sepsis. Their free helpline for those affected by sepsis can be reached on 0808 800 0029. Sepsis was the cause of Joy's death and so this charity is very close to my heart.

Marie Curie is a UK charity that provides palliative care and support for anyone living with a terminal illness and their families. Their helpline is free to call on 0800 090 2309 and their website has a range of resources offering practical and emotional support. I am fortunate to be a digital ambassador for them. They asked me to speak on a live panel event about a year after Joy died, and I saw just what great work they do. Since then I help to promote their work wherever I can.

Griefcast is a podcast that examines the human experience of grief and death – but with comedians, so it's cheerier than it sounds. I was honoured to be a guest on this podcast back in 2018 (episode 50, if you want to listen). Doing this made me realise just how important it was to speak openly about grief and also how important laughter can be as part of the healing process.

Widowed and Young (WAY) is a UK charity that offers a peer-to-peer support network for anyone who's lost a partner before their fifty-first birthday: widowedandyoung.org.uk. I was too old for them (!) but I have several friends who have joined.

Winston's Wish offers advice to young people and children after the death of a parent or sibling. I am also an ambassador for this wonderful charity who provide much needed support to families. Their helpline is free to call on 0808 802 0021 and offers therapeutic advice following a bereavement: winstonswish.org.

Sue Ryder is an online community for families and friends suffering bereavement or terminal illness: support.sueryder.org/community.

Child Bereavement UK supports children and young people up to the age of twenty-five who are facing bereavement, and anyone affected by the death of a child of any age: childbereavementuk.org.

Seek medical help urgently if you develop any or one of the following:

- Slurred speech or confusion
- Extreme shivering or muscle pain
- Passing no urine (in a day)
- Severe breathlessness
- It feels like you're going to die
- Skin mottled or discoloured

Just ask: 'Could it be sepsis?'
It's a simple question, but it could save a life.

Any child who:

- Is breathing very fast
- Has a 'fit' or convulsion
- Looks mottled, bluish or pale
- Has a rash that does not fade when you press it
- Is very lethargic or difficult to wake
- Feels abnormally cold to touch

Might have sepsis

Call 999 and ask: 'Could it be sepsis?'

The UK Sepsis Trust registered charity number (England & Wales) 1158843

Mental health

Samaritans
You can contact Samaritans 24 hours a day, 365 days a year. Call 116 123 (free from any phone), email jo@samaritans.org or visit some branches in person (check their website for details: samaritans.org).

SANEline
If you're experiencing a mental health problem or supporting someone else in mental distress, you can call SANEline on 0300 304 7000 (4.30 p.m.–10.30 p.m. every day).

Mind
The website mind.org.uk has a range of helpful information, from an A to Z of mental health to a supportive online community (for over-eighteens) elefriends.org.

The Big Draw is a visual literacy charity that promotes the universal language of drawing as a tool for learning, expression and invention: thebigdraw.org. I was honoured to be asked to be an ambassador for their 2019 campaign (Wellbeing Through Creativity) and am pleased to say that role is now permanent. With drawing being such a huge part of my life, this means an awful lot to me. I am a great believer in the healing power of art and creativity in general – as evident in this book – and love to see their work with families and communities.

Acknowledgements

A big thank you to the following people:

The lovely folk at John Murray (especially Abigail Scruby) for their belief in this book.

All my friends at the Archway Theatre, Horley, who were there for me from day one and continue to be a support today.

Joy's siblings: Chris, Geoff and Marie and their families. Gran'ma and Grandpa (Joy's mum and dad) for . . . well, everything really.

Karen and Steve, who spoil my kids rotten when I occasionally dump them there!

Pete, who moved on to my sofa the day after Joy died and refused to leave for about two weeks until he knew I would be OK!

Jane, my Northern soulmate and BFF.

Damh the Bard for Joy's beautiful Passing Ceremony and Eleanore for serenading her on her way.

Lily and Ben – who give my life purpose and make me so proud.

Above all, Joy – for all the love and laughter. My muse, my inspiration and my guide.

I guess that's normal life then...

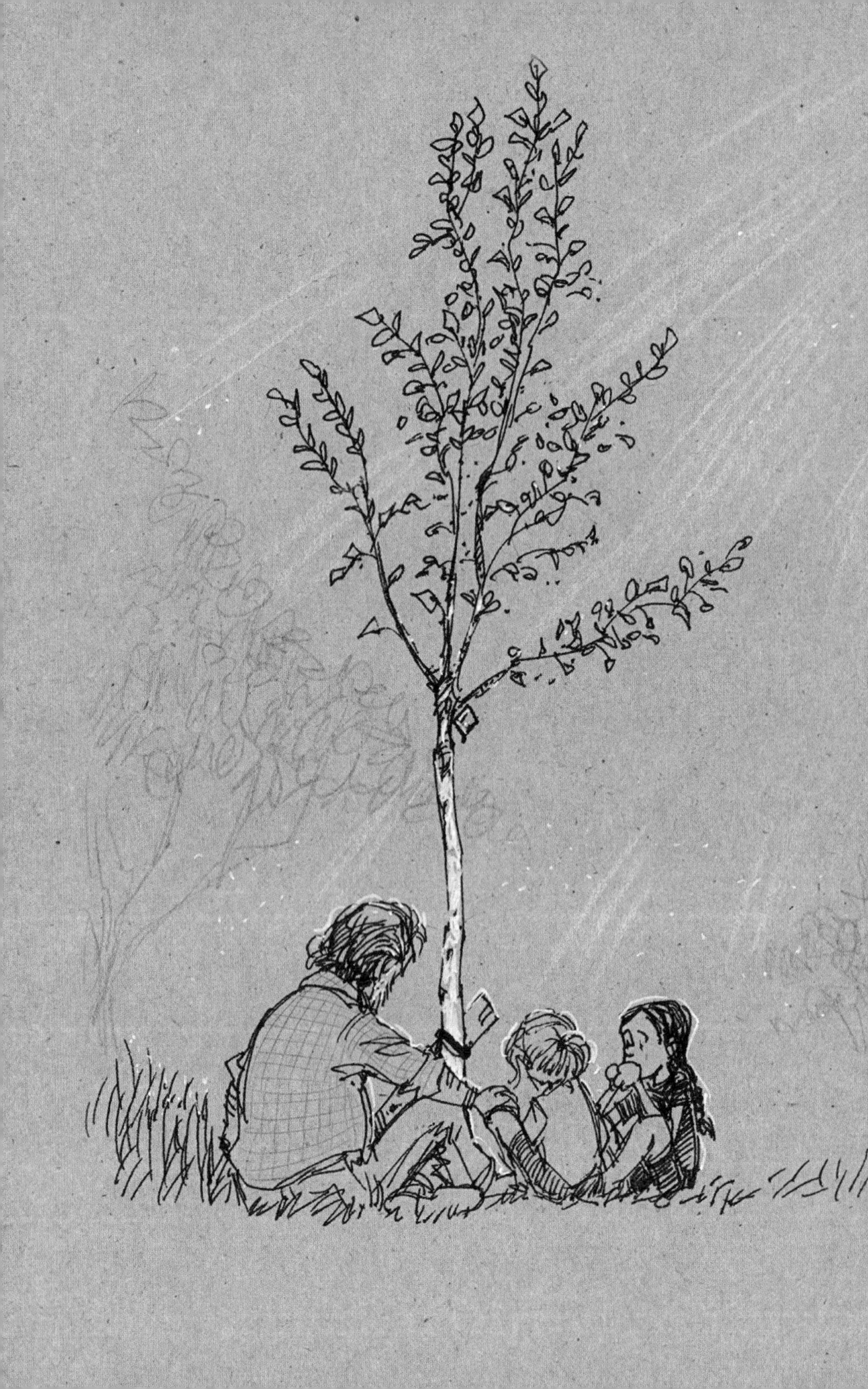